# DRIVING TOURS

# IRELAND

**PRENTICE HALL TRAVEL**

**New York • London • Toronto • Sydney • Tokyo • Singapore**

Written by Susan Poole and Lyn
Gallagher

Copy editor: Helen Douglas-Cooper

Edited, designed, produced and
distributed by AA Publishing,
Fanum House, Basingstoke,
Hampshire RG21 2EA.

© The Automobile Association
1992.

Maps © The Automobile
Association 1992.

Typesetting: Avonset, Midsomer
Norton, Nr Bath, Avon.

Colour origination: L. C. Repro &
Sons Ltd, Aldermaston, Reading.

Printed and bound in Italy by
Printers S.R.L., Trento.

The contents of this publication are
believed correct at the time of
printing. Nevertheless, the publishers
cannot accept responsibility for
errors or omissions, or for changes
in details given.

Every effort has been made to
ensure accuracy in this guide.
However, things do change and we
would welcome any information to
help keep the book up to date.

Published by AA Publishing.

Published in the United States by
Prentice Hall General Reference.

 A division of Simon &
Schuster, Inc., 15 Columbus
Circle, New York, NY 10023.

PRENTICE HALL and colophon are
registered trademarks of Simon &
Schuster, Inc.

ISBN 0-13-220443-6

Cataloging-in-Publication Data is
available from the Library of
Congress.

Title page: *Jarveys and traps at
Muckross*

Above: *Janus figure, Boa Island*

# CONTENTS

# INTRODUCTION

This book is not only a practical guide for the independent traveller, but is also invaluable for those who would like to know more about the country.

It is divided into 4 regions, each containing between 4 and 10 tours. The tours start and finish in the towns and cities which we consider to be the best centres for exploration. Each tour has details of the most interesting places to visit en route. Side panels cater for special interests and requirements and cover a range of categories – for those whose interest is in history, wildlife or walking, and those who have children. There are also panels which highlight scenic stretches of road along the route and which give details of special events, gastronomic specialities, crafts and customs. These are cross-referred back to the main text.

The simple route directions are accompanied by an easy-to-use map of the tour and there are addresses of local tourist information centres in some of the towns en route as well as in the start town.

Simple charts show how far it is from one town to the next in miles and kilometres. These can help you to decide where to take a break and stop overnight, for example. (All distances quoted are approximate.)

Before setting off it is advisable to check with the information centre at the start of the tour for recommendations on where to break your journey and for additional information on what to see and do, and when best to visit.

*The magnificent gardens and house of Mount Stewart, near Greyabbey, County Down*

## ENTRY REGULATIONS

No passport is needed if you are a British citizen born in the UK and travelling from Britain. Other EC visitors must have a passport or suitable identity documents. All other nationalities need a passport, and a very few need visas.

## CUSTOMS REGULATIONS

Standard EC customs regulations apply when travelling between the Republic or Northern Ireland and another EC country, and if crossing the border between the two. Travellers may import or export goods for their personal use, up to certain limits depending on whether the goods were bought in ordinary shops (tax paid) or duty-free shops.

## EMERGENCY TELEPHONE NUMBERS

In both the Republic and Northern Ireland, dial 999 for police, fire or ambulance.

## HEALTH

There are no special health requirements or regulations for visitors to the Republic or Northern Ireland. It is best to take out medical insurance, though EC visitors are covered by a reciprocal agreement. If you want to rely on this, you must bring Form E111 or equivalent with you – contact your post office for details.

## CURRENCY

The monetary units are (in the Republic) the Irish pound (punt), abbreviated as IR£, and (in Northern Ireland) the pound sterling (£), each divided into 100 pence. These are not interchangeable.

## CREDIT CARDS

In the Republic, cards carrying the Eurocard symbol and American Express and Diners cards are generally accepted, though not by some restaurants and smaller independent retailers and fuel stations. In Northern Ireland, cards other than the Eurocard type are of limited use outside the main towns. Personal cheques can be cashed using a Eurocheque card. When staying in B&B establishments, expect to pay cash.

## BANKS

Banks are the best place to change money. Normal opening hours are 10.00–12.30, 13.30–15.00 hrs (09.30–15.30 hrs in Northern Ireland), weekdays only. Some banks open on Saturday morning. Most banks in Dublin and Belfast stay open till 17.00 hrs on Thursdays. Foreign exchange counters in the main airports give decent rates: Belfast, open daily, 07.00–20.00 hrs (22.00 hrs on

Saturday and Sunday); Dublin, open 06.45–22.00 hrs in summer, 07.30–22.30 hrs in winter; Shannon, to service all flights; and Cork, open on weekdays all year and at weekends in summer.

## TIME

Both the Republic and Northern Ireland follow Greenwich Mean Time, but with clocks put forward one hour from late March to late October, as in Britain. Time differences with other countries are: Australia add eight to 10 hours; Canada subtract three and a half to nine hours; New Zealand add 12 hours; US subtract five to 11 hours.

## POST OFFICES

In the Republic, standard post office opening times are 09.00–17.30 hrs, Monday to Saturday, but sub-post offices close at 13.00 hrs one day a week. The General Post Office in O'Connell Street, Dublin, is open Monday to Saturday, 08.00–20.00 hrs

and 10.30–18.00 hrs on Sundays and bank holidays. Post boxes are green; Republic of Ireland stamps must be used.

In Northern Ireland, standard opening times are 09.00–17.30 hrs, Monday to Friday, and 09.00–12.30 hrs on Saturdays. Post boxes are red, and British stamps must be used.

## TELEPHONES

To call a number in Ireland, first dial the access code: Australia 0011; Canada 011; New Zealand 00; UK (for the Republic) 010. Then dial 353 for the Republic or 44 for Northern Ireland, and then the full number (omitting the first zero).

If calling a Dublin number from the UK: for a 6-digit number dial 010 353 12. For a 7-digit number omit the 2. Note: Dublin numbers are in the process of changing from 6 to 7 digits; if in doubt, ring Directory Enquiries.

For international calls out of Ireland except to Britain, dial 16 in the Republic or 010 in Northern Ireland, wait for a new tone, then dial the country code: Australia 16; Canada 1;

## EMBASSIES AND CONSULATES

Embassies in the Republic of Ireland:
Australia: Fitzwilton House, Wilton Terrace, Dublin 2 (tel: (01) 761 517)
Canada: 65 St Stephen's Green, Dublin 2 (tel: (01) 781 988)
UK: 31 Merrion Road, Dublin 4 (tel: (01) 695 211)
US: 42 Elgin Road, Dublin 4 (tel: (01) 688 777)
Consular offices for Northern Ireland:
Australia High Commission, Australia House, The Strand, London WC2B 4LA (tel: (071) 379 4334)
Canada High Commission, Macdonald House, 1 Grosvenor Square, London W1X 0AB (tel: (071) 629 9492
New Zealand High Commission, New Zealand House, Haymarket, London SW1Y 4TQ (tel: (071) 930 8422)
US: Queens House, 14 Queen Street, Belfast 1 (tel: (0232) 328 239).

## TOURIST OFFICES

Both the Irish Tourist Board (Bord Failte) and the Northern Ireland Tourist Board maintain offices abroad. These can supply a wide range of information to help you plan your visit, including brochures and guides, most of them free.

Irish Tourist Board (Bord Failte):
Australia: 5th Level, 36 Carrington Street, Sydney, NSW 2000 (tel: (02) 299 6177).
Canada: 160 Bloor Street, East Suite 934, Toronto, Ontario M4W 1B9 (tel: (416) 929 2777).
UK: 150 New Bond Street, London W1Y 0AQ (tel: (071) 493 3201); 53 Castle Street, Belfast BT1 1GH (tel: (0232) 327 888).
US: 757 Third Avenue, New York, NY 10017 (tel: (212) 418 0800).
Northern Ireland Tourist Board:
Republic of Ireland: 16 Nassau Street, Dublin 2 (tel: (01) 679 1977).
UK: Northern Ireland Business Centre, 11 Berkeley Street, London W1X 5AD (tel: (071) 493 0601)
US: Suite 500, 276 Fifth Avenue, New York, NY 1001 (tel: (212) 686 6250).

## ELECTRICITY

220 volts AC (50 cycles) is standard. Sockets for small appliances are the three-pin flat or two-pin round wall types.

## PUBLIC HOLIDAYS

(R) Republic only
(NI) Northern Ireland only
1 January – New Year's Day
17 March – St Patrick's Day
Good Friday and Easter Monday
1st Monday in May – May Day
Last Monday in May – Spring Bank Holiday (NI)
1st Monday in June – June Holiday (R)
12 July – Orangemen's Day (NI)
1st Monday in August – August Holiday (R)
Last Monday in August – Summer Holiday (NI)
Last Monday in October – October Holiday (R)
25 December – Christmas Day
26 December – St Stephen's Day (Boxing Day)

New Zealand 64; US 1. Then dial the full number omitting the first zero.

New-style glass and metal call boxes are replacing the old ones which are blue and cream in the Republic and red in Northern Ireland. Phones using cards (which can be bought at retail outlets such as newsagents) are also on the increase.

## MOTORING

### Documents

You will need a valid driving licence (with an English-language translation if you wish to rent a car) plus, if bringing a vehicle in, its registration book, with a letter of authorisation from the owner if he or she is not accompanying the vehicle. Your car, and any trailer, should carry a nationality sticker. In the Republic, you may not allow an Irish resident to drive your vehicle, other than a garage hand with your written permission.

Full comprehensive insurance cover is advisable. If you intend crossing the border, check that your insurance covers you in both the Republic and Northern Ireland.

### Route directions

Throughout the book the following abbreviations are used for roads:
M – motorways
R – regional roads
Northern Ireland only:
A – main roads
B – local roads
Republic of Ireland only:
N – national primary/secondary roads
T – trunk roads*
L – link roads*
* These classifications are gradually being phased out.

### Driving conditions

Drive on the left. In the Republic there are no motorways apart from short stretches north and west of Dublin. Potential hazards are loose chippings, livestock, and the relaxed attitude of Dublin drivers to red traffic lights. In Northern Ireland, the major roads are fast and well maintained, and seldom congested, though checkpoints are a potential cause of delay.

### Breakdowns

If the car is rented, contact the rental company. If it is your own car, and you are a member of the Automobile Association or one of the AIT (Alliance International de Tourisme) driving clubs, you can call on the AA rescue service (run by The Automobile Association of Ireland in the Republic). The RAC operates a similar service for its members but only in Northern Ireland.

### Car hire and fly/drive

Renting a car in the Republic is expensive compared to Northern Ireland, though rates vary; smaller local firms often offer cheaper deals than the large international companies but may not let you pick the car up in one place and return it in another. The national tourist boards can supply a list of companies. The cheapest method is to book a fly-drive or rail-ferry-drive inclusive package.

*A welcome respite in the busy little town of Macroom, a marketing centre for the surrounding area. Many pubs are the social centre for the traditional music, song and dance of Ireland*

*Ladies' View, named after Queen Victoria and her ladies-in-waiting*

## Speed limits

In the Republic the limits are 30mph (48kph) in built-up areas and 55mph (88kph) elsewhere unless otherwise indicated; for non-articulated vehicles with one trailer, the maximum is 40mph (64kph). In Northern Ireland, the limits are 30mph (48kph) in built-up areas, 60mph (96kph) in country areas, and 70mph (113kph) on dual carriageways and motorways, unless otherwise indicated; for trailers the maximum is usually 40mph (64kph).

## Accidents

Northern Ireland
In the event of an accident, the vehicle should be moved off the carriageway wherever possible. Hazard warning lights should be used if fitted. If available, a red triangle should be placed on the road at least 165 feet (50m) before the obstruction and on the same side of the road.

Republic of Ireland
If you are involved in an accident you must stop immediately and exchange particulars with the other party. If this is not possible you must report the accident to a member of the Garda Siochana or at the nearest Garda station.

*St Finbar's Hermitage, in remote Gougane Barra*

# MUNSTER

The province of Munster is made up of the counties of Waterford, Cork, Kerry, Limerick, Clare and Tipperary. Its fertile, ever-changing landscapes form, in essence, a microcosm of Ireland itself.

Soaring, surf-fringed cliffs rise above tiny coves set among long stretches of sandy beach. Ancient mountains, awash with the brilliant colours of rhododendrons and the delicate hues of heather, are slashed by deep gaps and scenic passes.

The Knockmealdown and Comeragh ranges guard east Munster, while to the west the peaks of Macgillycuddy's Reeks include Ireland's highest, 3,400-foot (1,036m) Carrantouhill. The Slieve Mish range marches out to the very tip of the Dingle Peninsula, and the Galtees, Slieve Felims, and Silvermines, straggle across the interior.

A variety of fish – salmon, brown trout, sea trout and coarse fish – fill Munster's rivers like the mighty Shannon that draws a watery line along the boundaries of counties Kerry, Clare, Limerick and Tipperary; the Lee that rises in the hills of Gougane Barra and flows eastward to split into two forks that flow around Cork city's island centre; the tidal Blackwater whose scenic beauty as it makes its way to the sea at Youghal has earned it the title of the unofficial 'Rhine of Ireland'; and the Suir, Slaney and Nire whose waters trace their way across the face of eastern Munster.

Fertile fields are ringed by stone walls and verdant woodlands. Small fishing villages along the coast and prosperous inland market towns dot the landscape. Three of Ireland's largest industrial cities and most important ports – Waterford, Cork and Limerick – ring the coastline, while inland lies the great Golden Plain of Tipperary.

Ancient ringforts, dolmens, and cairns pre-date recorded history, while massive castles, monasteries and round towers speak of Christians, Vikings and Normans. The stone promontory fort Dunbeg stands guard on the Dingle Peninsula as it has since before the dawn of history, while adjacent fields contain the still-intact beehive huts of early Christians. The lofty Rock of Cashel is a reminder of both the days of Celtic kings of Munster and the coming of Christianity, and nearby Cahir has a perfectly preserved 12th-century Norman castle.

The breathtaking scenery and the juxtaposition of history with modern progress leaves the visitor with an almost overwhelming sense of the enduring nature of the region. There is a feeling that time has not stood still in this ancient land, but is marching on into eternity, its past a solid foundation for the future.

## Tour 1 ✗

The strange barren landscape of the Burren is the most evocative sight of this region, though the towering grandeur of the Cliffs of Moher forms another unforgettable vista. For history lovers, Clare is a county of castles. Ennis, which readily claims the affection of the visitor, is the base for the tour.

## Tour 2

From the Viking city of Limerick, this tour takes you west along the banks of the Shannon estuary, tracing the footsteps of the mighty Desmond clan who left massive castles in their wake. The route turns south, where history merges with culture in northern County Kerry and continues east and north for medieval ruins in Newcastle West and the picturesque beauty of Adare.

## Tour 3

Turning east from Limerick city, it is not such a long way to Tipperary town, in the heart of that county's Golden Vale. Further east is the great Rock of Cashel, with its impressive ruins and folk village, then on to Thurles, Roscrea and Nenagh.

## Tour 4 ✗

Tralee is the gateway to a tour of the antiquities of the Dingle Peninsula, through tiny seaside villages and

over the breathtaking Connor Pass to Dingle town. Prehistoric forts, bee-hive huts and a drystone oratory that has stood watertight for over 1,000 years are only a few relics of this magical place.

*The Ring of Kerry, near Kells. This scenic road, clinging to the coast of the Iveragh Peninsula for much of its way, is one of the most picturesque in Ireland for its mountains and marine scenery*

### Tour 5

The 112-mile (180km) Ring of Kerry takes top billing on this tour as you travel from one scenic wonder to the next. Mountains, lakes, sandy beaches and offshore islands form an unforgettable panorama, and Killarney town has its own fair share of splendid lakes, antiquities and legends.

### Tour 6

From Kenmare, this tour takes you south to semi-tropical gardens at Glengarriff and the Italianate gardens on Garinish Island, reached by a short boat trip. It continues along wild seascapes and mountain passes of the Beara Peninsula.

### Tour 7

This tour takes you to Blarney to kiss the famous stone and northwest through historic towns before turn-ing east and south for Cahir's Norman castle, the spectacular drive across The Vee, Lismore's fairytale castle perched above the Blackwater river, and Youghal's harbour, haunted by Sir Walter Raleigh.

### Tour 8

Turning south and west from Cork, the splendours of West Cork unfold along this tour. Delightful little coves and sandy beaches are backed by wooded hills. A turn inland takes you through a mountain to remote Gougane Barra.

### Tour 9

After exploring historic Bantry, with its great house and attractive harbour, the route takes you to picturesque Skibbereen and Balti-more, a tiny village which has seen more than its share of violent events, and circles the unspoiled peninsula that stretches to Mizen Head, the southernmost mainland point of Ireland.

### Tour 10

Waterford is the starting point for a journey along dramatic coastal cliffs and coves, picturesque castles, panoramic mountain views, and lush farmland. The Vee opens up unfor-gettable views of heather-covered mountains and bogs and Tipperary's fertile landscape.

## 2/3 days – 159 miles (256km)

# CLARE

Ennis • Milltown Malbay • Lahinch • Cliffs of Moher
Ballyvaughan • Lisdoonvarna • Kilfenora and the Burren
Kinvarra • Quin • Bunratty • Ennis

The pleasant town of Ennis winds around low hills on both sides of the River Fergus. The *Cathedral* of the diocese of Killaloe was built in 1831, two years after Catholic emancipation. County Clare was at the forefront of this struggle and played a critical role in its success by electing Daniel O'Connell as Member of Parliament. A statue of O'Connell stands at the heart of the town. Another man who moulded the Irish nation is honoured in a memorial before the massive porticoed *Courthouse*. Eamon de Valera, who fought an election here in 1917 and went on to become Taoiseach (Prime Minister) and President, was a TD (MP) for the county. His life and influence are recorded in a museum which is housed in an award-winning conversion of a *Presbyterian church*. The *Franciscan abbey* in Ennis was a Protestant church in the early 19th century. Originally founded by the O'Brien family in the 13th century, and with subtle stone decoration, its most outstanding feature is the tall tapering east window.

The little resort of Milltown Malbay has an unspoilt charm, and makes a good base for exploring the Clare coastline

ℹ️ Clare Road

*Take the N85 for Lahinch. After 9 miles (14km) turn left at Inagh on to the R460 (L55) for Milltown Malbay. After another 9 miles (14km) turn right on to the R474 (L52) for Milltown Malbay.*

### Milltown Malbay, Co Clare

**1** The coastline of County Clare is better endowed with cliffs and rocky foreshore than with beaches, but there is good bathing at White (or Silver) Strand. Close by is **Spanish Point**, which owes its name to the unhappy fate of shipwrecked sailors from the Spanish Armada, executed by Sir Turlough O'Brien in 1588.

Milltown Malbay feels like a seaside resort, even though it is a little inland. It is an important centre for traditional music.

*Take the N67 for 7 miles (11km) to Lahinch.*

### Lahinch, Co Clare

**2** The busiest resort in Clare, the popularity of Lahinch derives from its splendid beach, good for bathing and popular for surfing. The name Lahinch comes from the Irish name for peninsula, as it has water on three sides. Its name today is perhaps most often associated with the championship golf course.

Across the bay lies **Liscannor**, birthplace of John Holland, the man who developed the submarine into a useful naval vessel in 1900. In appreciation, the US Navy erected a commemorative headstone at the small fishing harbour.

*Take the R478 (L54) 6 miles (10km) for the Cliffs of Moher.*

### RECOMMENDED WALKS

*Ennis, Co Clare* For an interesting historic walk, try the excellent town trail in Ennis.

**3** *Cliffs of Moher, Co Clare*
The best way to appreciate the full grandeur of the Cliffs of Moher is by foot. At the **Hags Head** there are sea arches and a cave to be seen, while from **O'Brien's Tower** the view extends from Kerry to Connemara. A Walking Guide for the path starting at O'Brien's Tower is available from the Visitor Centre.

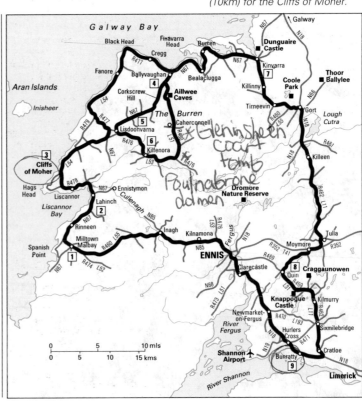

*O'Brien's Tower marks the northern end of the spectacular Cliffs of Moher*

## Cliffs of Moher, Co Clare

**3** These awe-inspiring bastions of rock rise sheer from the sea to a height of nearly 670 feet (200m) and run relentlessly for 5 miles (8km). The great Irish naturalist, Robert Lloyd Praeger, writing in the 1940s, suggested: 'If you want to feel very small, go out in one of the canvas curraghs on a day when a ground swell is coming in from the ocean, and get your boatman to row you along the base of those gigantic rock-walls. The rollers and their reflections from the cliffs produce a troubled sea on which your boat dances like a live thing, like a tiny cork, and the vast dark precipice above, vertical and in places overhanging, seems to soar up to the troubled sky. It is a wonderful experience.'

Generations of visitors have not failed to be impressed by the monumental quality of these cliffs. In 1835 Sir Cornelius O'Brien MP built **O'Brien's Tower** as an observation point for 'strangers visiting the Magnificent Scenery of this neighbourhood' on the highest point of the cliffs and overlooking a rockstack called Breanan Mor. Today's visitor has the advantage of a **Visitor Centre**, which has leaflets explaining the history and geology of the area, as well as giving information about walks and bird life.

ⓘ Visitor Centre

*Continue on the **R478 (L54)**, turning left to bypass Lisdoonvarna, and follow the coastal route, **R477 (L54)**, by Black Head to Ballyvaughan, 25 miles (40km).*

## Ballyvaughan, Co Clare

**4** Ballyvaughan is an attractive village, focused on a large harbour used for a small fishing fleet, for sailing and for boat trips to the islands. Close to the village is a cluster of holiday homes in traditional style, known as 'Rent an Irish Cottage', which is a popular feature of this area. Ballyvaughan is a centre for contemporary and traditional craftspeople.

*Take the **N67** up Corkscrew Hill for 10 miles (16km) to Lisdoonvarna.*

## Lisdoonvarna, Co Clare

**5** 'Matchmaking' has long been synonymous with Lisdoonvarna, and festivals are held to persuade traditionally reluctant bachelor farmers to the altar. The town has a great reputation for fun and good company, which is at its height in September when the harvest is gathered in. It also has Ireland's only active spa. The **Spa Centre** has a Pump House and health and recreational facilities.

*Take the **R476 (L53)** for 5 miles (8km) to Kilfenora.*

### FOR CHILDREN

**4** *Ballyvaughan, Co Clare*
The Burren is widely known for its potholes and caves but only experienced potholers can attempt to explore most of them. **Aillwee Caves**, south of Ballyvaughan, are perfect for a memorable family visit. Guided tours are informative and often amusing, and passages are safe and lit throughout. The reception building has been built to blend in with the remote and beautiful environment.

## BACK TO NATURE

Ireland's rarest and shyest wild animal, the beautiful pine marten, is now plentiful only in County Clare, its numbers drastically reduced in the last century because of the demand for its coat. A night hunter, it can occasionally be seen in the headlights of cars. A favoured haunt is **Dromore Nature Reserve**, 6 miles (10km) north of Ennis, a habitat of semi-natural woodland, and wetland that includes lake and marsh.

## SPECIAL TO...

Medieval banquets have become a very popular ingredient of many holidays in the Shannonside region. In the atmospheric surroundings of Bunratty, Knappogue or Dunguaire, medieval feasts or banquets are served with pageantry, costume, music and rhyme, with the emphasis on plenty of fun. The history of the castle dictates the mood and content of each entertainment.

## Kilfenora and the Burren, Co Clare

**6** You will already have passed through part of the Burren, but here at Kilfenora, the **Burren Display Centre** puts this unique landscape and its plants into context. May is the best time to see the wild rock garden of flowers that covers the Burren, crowding together in crevices or covering the limestone outcrops in profusion. It is not only the abundance of the plants that makes the Burren so special, as bright blue gentians blossom in the shallow turf, and mountain avens, clear white with golden centres, tumble across the limestone terraces. The Burren also harbours a profusion of rare varieties. Species normally found only in the Arctic or at high altitude, such as alpine saxifrage, appear in the Burren, and so does the dense-flowered orchid, which is a Mediterranean plant. Twenty-two varieties of orchid grow here, favouring a unique ecosystem created by a combination of factors, including fast drainage into the limestone, mild, moist weather conditions, the absence of grasses and the control of hazel scrub by goats. The Burren may be a botanist's paradise, but the grey shimmering contours of this strange and lonely landscape will leave an impression on all who see it.

*The Burren is a unique natural rock-garden landscape*

*Take the Corofin road, **R476** (**L53**) for 4 miles (6km), then turn left on to the **R480** (**L51**) for Ballyvaughan. Turn right and follow the **N67** to Kinvarra.*

### Kinvarra, Co Galway

**7** Kinvarra is a fishing village in Galway Bay, and the hill above gives splendid views of these much loved Irish waters. **Dunguaire Castle** – the 7th-century seat of the King of Connacht, Guaire Aidhneach, a man of celebrated hospitality – stands on a promontory in Kinvarra Bay. The 17th-century tower house and bawn that now stands here was built by his descendants, the O'Heynes.

South of Kinvarra, near Gort, is **Thoor Ballylee**, where Yeats lived and which came to be symbolic to the poet. You can climb the 'narrow winding stair', and see an audio-visual presentation on Yeats' life and times. Yeats often visited **Coole Park**, home of Lady Gregory, co-founder of the Abbey Theatre. The house, where many of the figures involved in the literary renaissance met, was demolished in 1941, but the beautiful woods of which Yeats wrote, are in state care.

*Turn right for Gort. After 4 miles (6km) bear left, and go through Tirneevin to Gort. Take the **N18** for Ennis and after 6 miles (10km) follow the **R462 (L11)** for Tulla. Half a mile (1km) further on, turn right on to the **R352 (T41)** for Ennis, and then after 2 miles (3km) turn left for Quin, a total distance of 33 miles (53km).*

## Quin, Co Clare

**8** A Franciscan friary, of which altars and tombs, a graceful tower and cloister remain, was built by the MacNamaras in the 15th century, on the site of a 13th-century castle. It also incorporates the buildings of a large Anglo-Norman castle. Close by **Knappogue Castle**, is typical of hundreds of medieval castles that are scattered throughout Clare, many of them, like the 1467 **tower house** at Quin, the preserve of the MacNamara family. The present castle has Georgian and Regency extensions. Set in pretty gardens, rising from a well-planted demesne, it combines the atmosphere of sturdy stronghold and comfortable home.

Craggaunowen is close to Quin, too. An enterprising historical project has been built up around **Craggaunowen Castle**, a 16th-century tower house which has been completely restored and displays replicas of furniture and tools of the period. The Project lifts the lid off many of the skills of the past, including the construction of daub-and-wattle buildings, and weaving and cooking techniques. There is a reconstruction of a *crannóg*, or defensive lake dwelling, used by the Celts in the 6th or 7th century. Another replica, that of the boat St Brendan the Navigator is said to have used when he discovered America in the 6th century, is on display. In 1977, in a journey that captured the imagination, Tim Severin sailed the Atlantic in this replica to show that Brendan's voyage would have been possible.

*Take the road to Limerick, **R469 (L31)**, turning right after 4 miles (6km) on to the **R462 (L11)**. After 6 miles (10km) turn right on to the **N18** for Ennis and Bunratty.*

*The replica of the boat in which St Brendan the Navigator is said to have sailed to America*

*Fifteenth-century Bunratty Castle houses a fine collection of medieval art, furniture and weaponry*

## Bunratty, Co Clare

**9** One of Ireland's most popular tourist destinations, Bunratty's completely restored Norman-Irish keep sits four-square by the main road, its stout defences, including three 'murder holes' over the main door, defying entry. In fact, this is the most inviting of castles and, furnished with Lord Gort's magnificent medieval collection, it gives a colourful insight into the life of a 15th-century keep. In the grounds is **Bunratty Folk Park**, which re-creates 19th-century life, both in the small cottages and houses of the region, and in a village street. The scenes are enlivened with traditional crafts in action – bread-making, candle-making, thatching, milling and basket-weaving. **Ballycasey Craft Workshops** for contemporary craftsmen and women are close by.

Towards Limerick is **Cratloe**, where a mighty oak forest once supplied the timbers for Westminster Hall in London and the Grianan in Ulster. The woods here are still important. **Cratloe Woods House**, a good example of the Irish longhouse dating from the 17th century, is the family home of descendants of the O'Briens.

ⅈ Folk Park

*Take the **N18** for 14 miles (23km) back to Ennis.*

| | |
|---|---|
| Ennis – Milltown Malbay | **20 (32)** |
| Milltown Malbay – Lahinch | **7 (11)** |
| Lahinch – Cliffs of Moher | **6 (10)** |
| Cliffs of Moher – Ballyvaughan | **25 (40)** |
| Ballyvaughan – Lisdoonvarna | **10 (16)** |
| Lisdoonvarna – Kilfenora | **5 (8)** |
| Kilfenora – Kinvarra | **26 (42)** |
| Kinvarra – Quin | **33 (53)** |
| Quin – Bunratty | **13 (21)** |
| Bunratty – Ennis | **14 (23)** |

### FOR HISTORY BUFFS

From the little roads which cross the Burren north of Kilfenora much of archaeological interest can be found within a very small area. There are stone forts at **Caherconnell** and **Caherballykinvarga**. An ancient monastic site stands at **Noughaval**. At **Poulawack** is a cairn, thought to be Bronze Age, and there is a portal dolmen at **Poulnabrone**

In **Gleninsheen wedge tomb** a sheet-gold ribbed gorget, or crescent-shaped collar, dating from the 8th century BC, was found. Of the finest quality and workmanship, it was recognised as a national treasure and is held in the National Museum.

### SCENIC ROUTES

The descent to Ballyvaughan provides a wonderful combination of the extraordinary Burren rock formations with the little village of Ballyvaughan, its whitewashed cottages and harbour and the wide expanse of Galway Bay beyond. Kinvarra and Finavarra Head are to the right, Gleninagh Mountain and Black Head to the left.

**2 days – 112 miles (179km)**

# RIVER SHANNON RAMBLES

Limerick ● Askeaton ● Foynes ● Glin ● Tarbert
Ballybunion ● Listowel ● Abbeyfeale ● Newcastle West
Rathkeale ● Adare ● Limerick

The Celts were the first to recognise Limerick's strategic position when they built an earthen fort at the lowest ford of the River Shannon. In the 18th century the city developed its present form, and after a period of decline in the 20th century, a massive renovation programme has restored much of its earlier style.

*King John's Castle*, at Thomond Bridge, tops the list of attractions. Its excellent visitors' centre presents informative exhibits on the city past and present. *St Mary's Cathedral*, at Nicholas and Bridge streets, founded in the late 12th century by the King of Munster, is filled with fine antiquities. There are splendid panoramic views from its bell tower, and an excellent *Son et Lumiere* show is presented during summer months. (See also Tour 3.)

*The pretty thatched cottages and colourful gardens that line the broad main street of Adare give the village its old-world charm*

*i* Arthur's Quay

*Take the **N69** west for 17 miles (27km) to Askeaton.*

## Askeaton, Co Limerick

**1** A Middle Age stronghold of the Desmond clan, Askeaton sits on the River Deel in the very centre of the village. Alive with echoes of the past, ruined **Desmond Castle** inhabits a rocky islet in the village centre. Its last defending Earl of Desmond fled to the Kerry Hills when the castle and the town fell to British troops in 1580. The impressive Great Banqueting Hall measures 90 feet by 30 feet (28m by 9m) with windows set back to provide for window seats and vaulted rooms underneath. At the south end there is a small chapel.

On the east bank of the river, cloisters enclosed by black marble pointed arches and supported by cylindrical columns are relics of a 15th-century **Franciscan friary**.

*Follow the **N69** for 7 miles (11km) to Foynes.*

## Foynes, Co Limerick

**2** The most scenic portion of the coastal drive along the Shannon begins in this small seaport, though these days, its waters play host to luxury yachts as well as commercial ships. The first steamship to depart its docks was a blockade runner

*The medieval King John's Castle, Limerick, with a twin-towered gatehouse and curtain walls*

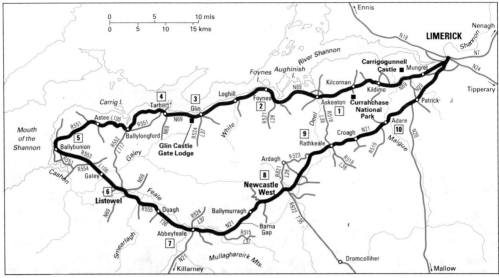

providing uniforms made in Limerick for Confederate forces during the American Civil War. During the late 1930s and 1940s, Foynes was the home port for a transatlantic sea plane service, and the **Flying Boat Museum** presents an audio-visual show along with mementoes of those pioneering days in the world of air travel.

*Continue west on the N69 for another 8 miles (13km) to Glin.*

### Glin, Co Limerick

**3** The Fitzgeralds, powerful Earls of Desmond, also dominated this village, and ruins of their **Castle of Glin** still overlook the Shannon estuary. It was fiercely defended in 1600 but fell to the English forces after two days of intense fighting. The Desmond holdings here have passed without interruption for more than seven centuries to the present Knight of Glin, whose home, **Glin Castle**, is a rather plain white building adorned by Gothic details and battlements that were added after its 1780s construction. It sits well off the road in

*Eighteenth-century Glin Castle. The decorative battlements were added during the 19th century*

a large demesne and is not open to the general public, although it is available to paying guests during selected months.

About 1 mile (1.5km) west of the village, look for the Gothic-style **Glin Castle Gate Lodge**, a pleasant tea-room and craft shop, where cast-offs from the castle are often scattered among craft items.

The castellated building over-looking Glin pier is **Hamilton's Tower**, a 19th-century 'folly' built by one Dr Hamilton to give employment to Irish famine victims.

*Continue west on the N69 for about 4 miles (6km) to Tarbert.*

### Tarbert, Co Kerry

**4** A car ferry across the Shannon to Killimer in County Clare departs the wooded headland that juts into the river's estuary at this quiet little village, a real timesaver for travellers who want to avoid Limerick traffic.

**BACK TO NATURE**

*Limerick, Co Limerick* About 11 miles (18km) west of Limerick on the **N69**, turn south for 2 miles (3km) on a signposted, unclassified road to reach **Currahchase National Park**. This was the estate of poet Aubrey de Vere (1814–1922). The grounds contain fine landscaped gardens and an arboretum with exotic plants, as well as the tombstone that marks his pet cemetery. A nature trail leads through the estate, one of the finest in Ireland, past native Irish trees and plants, and the picnic area is an ideal spot for lunching in the open.

**1** *Askeaton, Co Limerick* The southern banks of the Shannon estuary between Askeaton and Aughinish are the most important areas of the water system for wildfowl and waders. Look for curlews, bar-tailed godwits, wigeon, teal and scaup, which are best in autumn and winter.

## SCENIC ROUTES

The coast road **(N69)** from Foynes to Tarbert along the southern banks of the Shannon is one of the most enticing riverside drives in Ireland, with sweeping views of the river estuary. Adjacent to the village of Foynes, there is a layby with a picnic site, scenic viewpoints of the Shannon, and forest walks.

Rather different views are found at **Barna Gap**, a little over 7 miles (11km) southwest of Newcastle West on the **N21**. From roads crossing the ridge there are dramatic panoramic vistas of the great plain that runs eastward to the Galtee mountains, and viewing platforms are provided at the Gap. To the north and west, there are high moors and young forests.

## FOR CHILDREN

**5** *Ballybunion, Co Kerry*
The attractive beaches at the lively resort of Ballybunion will send the children splashing into the Atlantic waves. Surfing is a popular sport here, along with swimming. In addition, there are fascinating caves in the seaside cliffs to be explored at low tide with extreme caution and in the company of adults. In the town itself, there are several amusement parks with rides, swings and slides, as well as arcades with computer games.

## FOR HISTORY BUFFS

*Limerick, Co Limerick* The city's history comes to life in **King John's Castle**. Built in the 13th century as an instrument of royal authority and a military stronghold, it has been converted into an international visitors' centre. The centre presents an audio-visual overview of Limerick's long history, and contains historical exhibits and archaeological remains covering a timespan of some 800 years. Discovered at sub-floor level in 1990, the archaeological treasures are accessible to visitors even as the digs go on.

On the **N69**, about 3 miles (5km) west of Limerick, near the village of **Mungret**, there is a signposted turnoff to the ruins of **Carrigogunnell Castle**. The large, 14th-century castle was heavily fortified, but was blown up in 1691 during the second siege of Limerick. The views from its high, rocky perch are spectacular.

*Take the unclassified coastal road to Ballylongford, then the **R551 (L105)** to Ballybunion.*

### Ballybunion, Co Kerry

**5** The ruins of **Ballybunion Castle** stand on Castle Green in this popular Atlantic coast resort town. It is the fine beach, however, that draws visitors, as well as the network of **souterrains** (subterranean passages) near Castle Green and invigorating clifftop walks.

Just north of the town, the remains of a **promontory fort** overlook **Doon Cove**. The 18-hole golf course entices amateurs and professionals alike.

*Continue for 10 miles (16km) southeast via the **R553 (L106)** to Listowel.*

### Listowel, Co Kerry

**6** The castle in this bustling market town was the last to hold out against Elizabethan forces in the Desmond rebellion. When it fell in 1600, the entire garrison was put to the sword. Two Gothic-style churches dominate the town square, and the old Protestant church has been converted into an interesting **arts centre**. Take a look at a wonderful bit of plaster fantasy, the 'Maid of Erin' figure on the Central Bar that sits on one corner of the square. A local craftsman, Pat McAuliffe, and his son were creators of the lady and several other works around the town and in Abbeyfeale.

It was from a window of the Listowel Arms Hotel on the square that Charles Stewart Parnell, campaigner for Home Rule, made one of his last public appearances just three weeks before his death in 1891. Fans of the noted playwright John B Keane should head for his pub in William

*The excellent golf course at Ballybunion provides good views of the Atlantic*

Street, where he is often to be found mingling with the locals, or engaged in the storytelling for which he is famous. Lord Kitchener, of Khartoum fame, was born 4 miles (6km) north-west of town at **Gunsborough** in 1850.

*Take the **R555 (T36)** southeast for 11 miles (18km) to Abbeyfeale.*

### Abbeyfeale, Co Limerick

**7** In the foothills of the Mullaghhareirk Mountains, this little market town grew from the Cistercian abbey founded here in 1188. The only traces of the abbey have since been incorporated into the Catholic church building. The town square has a statue of Father William Casey, parish priest and leader of the tenant farmers' fight against landlordism in the mid and late 1800s.

Abbeyfeale pubs are often the venue for traditional music, song and dance.

*Take the **N21** northeast for 13 miles (21km) to Newcastle West.*

### Newcastle West, Co Limerick

**8** Adjacent to the town square of this bustling market town are the ruins of a **Knights Templar castle** dating from 1184. Burned in 1642, its two 15th-century halls, peel tower, keep, bastion and curtain wall have survived. While the Great Hall is largely in ruins, the Desmond Banqueting Hall is almost perfectly preserved, complete right down to a vaulted basement, and now serves as a cultural centre for recitals, concerts, lectures and exhibitions.

*Adare Manor, begun in 1832, was once the home of the Dunravens*

You can see Irish Dresden porcelain being made at the factory and showroom in **Dromcolliher**, some 9 miles (15km) southeast of town via the R522 (T36).

*Follow the N21 northeast for 8 miles (13km) to Rathkeale.*

### Rathkeale, Co Limerick

**9** The poet, Edmund Spenser and Sir Walter Raleigh first met in Rathkeale at **Castle Matrix**, built in 1440 and so named after an ancient Celtic sanctuary that once occupied this site. Now open to the public, the castle has furnishings authentic to its era and an outstanding library with many rare books. There is also a unique collection of documents dealing with the so-called 'Wild Geese', Irish chieftains and soldiers who fled the country to fight with European armies in the 17th and 18th centuries.

*Continue for 7 miles (11km) northeast via the N21 to Adare.*

### Adare, Co Limerick

**10** With its neat thatched cottages and broad main street, Adare is likely to come closer to the romantic image of the 'quaint little Irish village' than any other in the country, although its appearance is decidedly English. Credit for its beauty must go to the third Earl of Dunraven, who had a passion for early Irish architecture and local improvements.

The ancestral home of the Dunravens, **Adare Manor**, stands at the northern edge of town and is now a luxury hotel. In the heart of the hotel's golf course are the ruins of a **castle** on the banks of the River Maigue, a **Franciscan friary** dating back to 1464 and the 15th-century Desmond family **chapel** (check with the golf club before visiting).

In the village itself, remains of a 14th-century **Augustinian friary** sit near the fine, 14-arch bridge across the river. Its choir was taken over as a Church of Ireland parish church in 1875 by the Earl of Dunraven. Its refectory became a school, and the cloisters were put to use as a mausoleum. The complex is now open to the public.

*Take the N21, then turn left on to the N20 for 10 miles (16km) back to Limerick.*

| Route | miles (km) |
|---|---|
| Limerick – Askeaton | **17 (27)** |
| Askeaton – Foynes | **7 (11)** |
| Foynes – Glin | **8 (13)** |
| Glin – Tarbert | **4 (6)** |
| Tarbert – Ballybunion | **17 (27)** |
| Ballybunion – Listowel | **10 (16)** |
| Listowel – Abbeyfeale | **11 (18)** |
| Abbeyfeale – Newcastle West | **13 (21)** |
| Newcastle West – Rathkeale | **8 (13)** |
| Rathkeale – Adare | **7 (11)** |
| Adare – Limerick | **10 (16)** |

### RECOMMENDED WALKS

**5** *Ballybunion, Co Kerry*
Magnificent seascapes add to the exhilaration of clifftop walks from Ballybunion to Doon Point north of the strand. To the south is Doon Cove. The cliffs are riddled with fine caves, and although those at sea level are safe enough to explore at low tide, extreme caution should be observed when approaching the higher ones.

### SPECIAL TO ...

**6** *Listowel, Co Kerry*
Listowel is host to hordes of aspiring writers, poets and playwrights during its **Writers' Week**, held annually in late May or early June. The town has spawned such noted authors as John B Keane, Bryan MacMahon, George Fitzmaurice and Maurice Walsh, and the week of workshops, lectures and theatre productions was founded as a means for successful wordsmiths to give beginners the benefit of their experience and expertise. A must for budding writers.

2/3 days – 157 miles (253km)

# ANCIENT CASTLES & LAKE ODYSSEY

Limerick • Tipperary • Cashel • Thurles • Roscrea
Nenagh • Portumna • Mountshannon
Killaloe • Limerick

Limerick is an important commercial and industrial centre, with Shannon International Airport some 15 miles (24km) to the west. Among its many interesting attractions (see Tour 2) is the *Dominican Church* in Baker Place, whose 17th-century statue of Our Lady of Limerick contrasts sharply with the chancel's modern fresco.

The *Limerick Museum* in St John's Square exhibits relics from the Stone Age through each era of the city's history. Irish artists star at the *City Gallery of Art* in Pery Square, and the famous Limerick Lace is made at the *Good Shepherd Convent* in Clare Street. *The Granary*, in Michael Street, houses a pub and a restaurant. Cultural events, art exhibitions and theatrical productions are held in the *Belltable Arts Centre*, O'Connell Street. Guided walking tours leave from the Treaty Stone daily in the summer and there are good river walks on both banks of the Shannon.

## FOR HISTORY BUFFS

*Limerick, Co Limerick* Eleven miles (17.5km) northwest of Limerick via the **N18** west, then north on the **R462** to **Sixmilebridge**, is the **Craggaunowen Project**, a fascinating historical complex. There is a superb example of a 16th-century fortified house, and the adjacent lake holds a reconstructed *crannóg*, a prehistoric dwelling built on an artificial island. Housed in a glass structure nearby, the tiny leather boat *St Brendan* is an exact replica of the vessel in which the saint crossed the Atlantic in AD700 and was used by Tim Severin and his modern-day crew to retrace the legendary voyage.

**3** *Thurles, Co Tipperary*
Two rectangular keeps, remnants of the two Butler castles in Thurles, are reminders of the town's turbulent past. In the 10th century, the Irish and Norse fought fierce battles here, and when Strongbow's Anglo-Norman troops attacked in 1174, the Irish initially repelled them, but were unable to prevent their building a castle to control traffic on the River Suir.

*The circular keep of Nenagh Castle is one of the finest in Ireland. It was originally part of a larger castle built in the early 1200s*

[i] Arthur's Quay

*Take the **N24** southeast for 25 miles (40km) to Tipperary.*

## Tipperary, Co Tipperary

**1** A detour via the N24, 3 miles (5km) east of Limerick, takes you to Plassy, where there is a collection of more than 1,000 Irish antiquities and examples of medieval art at the **Institute for Higher Education**.

In the heart of Ireland's fertile Golden Vale, Tipperary town is an important dairy farming centre. It figured prominently in the 19th-century Land League campaigns to legalise land ownership for Irish tenants, and today is a thriving market town, and an excellent base for hill walking in the nearby Slievenamuck and Galtee mountains. The major point of interest in town is **St Michael's Church**, Gothic in design and noteworthy for its fine lancet windows and west door.

About 8 miles (13km) north of town via the **R497 (L34)** and **R505 (L111)**, the well-preserved circular keep of **Ballysheeda Castle** stands on a hillside 1 mile (1.5km) north of **Annacarty** village. Six miles (10km) south of Tipperary via the **R664** is the beautiful **Glen of Aherlow** (see Tours 10 and 14).

*Follow the **N74** for 12 miles (19km) to Cashel.*

*Tipperary town is surrounded by a broad plain of rich farmland that is bordered by mountains to north and south. Hunting, fishing and walking are popular activities in the region*

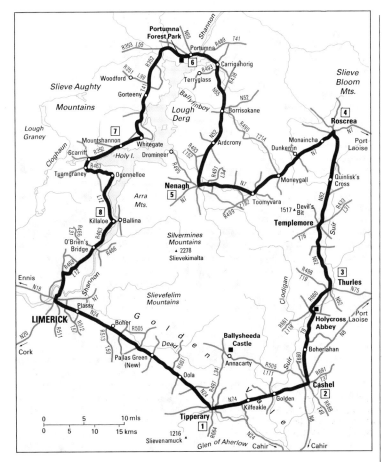

### Cashel, Co Tipperary

**2** Ecclesiastical ruins on the Rock of Cashel dominate the town of Cashel (see Tour 10), but also of interest are the Cashel Folk Village, and the ruins of the Dominican friary, which was rebuilt in 1480 after destruction by fire, both in Chapel Lane. Be sure to see the lovely 13th-century east window. The Bishop's Palace, set in enclosed grounds on Main Street, was built for Protestant archbishops and is a splendid example of 18th-century architecture. Now a hotel, it is a perfect place for a meal in the restaurant or more modest fare in the Bishop's Buttery.

*Take the R660 (T9) north for 13 miles (21km) to Thurles.*

### Thurles, Co Tipperary

**3** It was in the Hayes Hotel in this old Anglo-Norman town that the Gaelic Athletic Association was founded in 1884, which makes it virtually akin to a religious site in the eyes of many Irish sports fans. Bridge Castle, at the western end of the Suir river bridge, and Black Castle, near the town square, are remnants of Butler clan castles. The 19th-century Catholic Cathedral was built on the foundations of a medieval Carmelite settlement and the lavish use of marble, especially in the altars, gives a special beauty to its interior.

Holycross Abbey, a 12th-century Cistercian centre, is set on the east bank of the Suir 4 miles (6km) southwest of Thurles. Long abandoned and roofless, it has been restored as the active parish church.

*Take the N62 north for 21 miles (34km) to Roscrea.*

### Roscrea, Co Tipperary

**4** This pleasant market town is a good base for climbing and hill walking in the nearby Devil's Bit and Slieve Bloom mountains. Its most outstanding attraction is the Roscrea Heritage Centre in an annexe to Damer House, a town house dating from the early 18th century, set within the walls of an 11th-century Norman castle and narrowly saved from demolition in the mid-1970s. There are panoramic views from the top of the gate tower and, inside, the magnificently carved staircase is stunning. The house is lavishly decorated and furnished and holds paintings, furniture and interesting mementoes of life in the town through the ages.

Available from the Heritage Centre is a self-guided walking tour booklet that takes you by the ruins of St Cronan's Church and Round Tower, dating from the 12th century and a 12th-century High Cross.

At Monaincha, 2 miles (3km) southwest of town, the remains of a 12th-century church with 16th-century additions and an elegant High Cross are relics of a monastic settlement.

*Take the N7 southwest for 20 miles (32km) to Nenagh.*

### Nenagh, Co Tipperary

**5** Originally a Norman settlement, Nenagh served as a mid-19th-century garrison town, and finally evolved into a prosperous market town with many traditional shopfronts. One of the town's major features is the circular keep of Nenagh Castle, a mostly 1860 structure incorporating portions of a large castle built in the early 1200s by

the first Butler of Ormonde. The
100-foot-high (30m), 53-foot-wide
(16m) keep, with walls up to 20 feet
(6m) thick, formed part of the curtain
wall of the earlier castle. Winding
stairs set into the thickness of the wall
lead to the roof.

Nenagh's **Heritage Centre** is
located just across the road from the
castle in the old Governor's House
and county gaol. There is a
marvellous 'Lifestyles in Northwest
Tipperary' exhibition, as well as
visiting art and photograph exhibits.
**Nenagh Friary**, in Abbey Street, was
founded in about 1250 and still has a
13th-century church.

Six miles (10km) northwest of
Nenagh, via the R494 (L152) then the
R495, **Dromineer**, on the shores of
Lough Derg, is a lively fishing, sailing
and watersports centre.

*Head north on the **N52**, then left
on to the **N65** for 19 miles
(31km) to reach Portumna.*

## Portumna, Co Galway

**6** This small lakeside town at the
northern end of Lough Derg is a
popular fishing centre for the lake and
the River Shannon, as well as a major
base for cruisers. The impressive
ruins of **Portumna Castle** stand in its
demesne, laid out as an attractive
forest park, on the edge of town. Built
in 1609 by the Earl of Clanricarde, it
was destroyed by fire in 1826, but has
been restored and is open to the
public. Of special interest are the
Renaissance doorway with gunholes
on one side, the Jacobean gables on
the roof, and the square towers at
each corner.

About 7 miles (11km) south of
Portumna via the N65 and the R493
(L152), the village of **Terryglass**, on
the shores of Lough Derg, has a lovely
old stone church and the ruins of a
13th-century castle. There are boats
for hire and picnic facilities.

*Turn south on the **R352 (T41)** to
follow the shores of Lough Derg
for 17 miles (27km) to
Mountshannon.*

## Mountshannon, Co Clare

**7** The River Shannon, in the course
of its 230-mile (370km) rambles,
forms several lakes, of which **Lough
Derg** is the largest, stretching some
25 miles (40km) in length and

*Island-strewn Lough Derg is the
prettiest of the Shannon lakes and
provides good trout fishing*

sprinkled with numerous islands and
islets. The drive down its western
shore is delightful, with the lake in
view much of the way and never
more than a short detour to the east.
At the little town of Mountshannon,
hire a boat at the pier to visit the Holy
Island of **Iniscealtra** and its remains of
an early Christian settlement,
including no less than five churches
and a round tower.

*Continue southwest on the **R352
(T41)** to Tuamgraney, then turn
southeast on to the **R463 (L12)** to
reach Killaloe.*

## Killaloe, Co Clare

**8** In this charming little harbour
village on an elevated site that
once housed Kincora, the palace of Irish
king Brian Boru and his O'Brien
descendants, visit **St Flannan's Catholic
Church**. In the church grounds,
**St Molua's Oratory**, estimated to be
1,000 to 1,200 years old, reposes in
safety after being rescued when its
Friar's Island home was threatened
by submersion in a hydroelectric
development. The 12th-century
Church of Ireland **St Flannan's
Cathedral** is noteworthy for its
ornately carved Irish Romanesque
doorway, and it holds an ogham
(ancient Celtic writing) stone that also
has runic writings and a crude crucifix
believed to be formed by a Viking who
had been converted to Christianity. St
Flannan was the patron saint of this
diocese. Traces of a **ringfort** can be
seen on the southeastern side of a
steep hill known as Crag or Cragliath.

Fishing, boating and watersports
are the main preoccupations in
Killaloe, and lake cruises run in
summer months.

*Follow the **R463 (L12)** southwest
for 14 miles (23km) to return to
Limerick.*

| | |
|---|---|
| Limerick – Tipperary | **25 (40)** |
| Tipperary – Cashel | **12 (19)** |
| Cashel – Thurles | **13 (21)** |
| Thurles – Roscrea | **21 (34)** |
| Roscrea – Nenagh | **20 (32)** |
| Nenagh – Portumna | **19 (31)** |
| Portumna – Mountshannon | **17 (27)** |
| Mountshannon – Killaloe | **16 (26)** |
| Killaloe – Limerick | **14 (23)** |

**2/3 days – 97 miles (156km)**

# BEEHIVE HUTS & COASTAL SPLENDOURS

*One of the best-known and most colourful pubs in Dingle*

ℹ️ Ashe Hall, Denny Street

*Take the **R559 (T68)** west, with the Slieve Mish mountains on your left, to the little village of Camp.*

## Camp, Co Kerry

**1** In the village, turn off the main road west towards the mountains to reach James Ashe's pub, the epitome of everyone's image of what an old-time Irish pub should be – smoke-darkened wood, low ceilings, a peat fire glowing on the hearth, and the Ashe family carrying on a generations-old tradition.

*Go back for ½ mile (1km) before turning left on to the **R560** west to Castlegregory.*

## Castlegregory, Co Kerry

**2** There are fine beaches at Castlegregory, which sits at the neck of a spit of land dividing Tralee and Brandon bays, as well as all along the drive from Camp. Birdwatchers will want to turn left just before reaching the town to visit Lough Gill bird sanctuary, which has attracted such exotic species as the Bewick's swan from Siberia.

*Turn back east on the **R560**, then right on to the unclassified road signposted 'Dingle, Connor Pass'.*

## Connor Pass, Co Kerry

**3** Climbing between the Brandon and central Dingle groups of mountains, this 6-mile (10km) drive passes through some of Ireland's most spectacular scenery. On a fine day, there are vast panoramas of mountains, sea, lakes and valleys – on a not-so-fine day, mist and clouds can turn the narrow, winding road into a real driving challenge.

*The Connor Pass*

Tralee • Camp • Castlegregory • Connor Pass • Dingle
Ventry • Dunbeg • Fahan • Slea Head • Dunquin
Ballyferriter • Gallarus Oratory • Anascaul • Inch
Castlemaine • Tralee

**B**est known these days for its *Rose of Tralee* festival in late August, Tralee is the chief town of County Kerry, an important business centre and the principal gateway for the Dingle Peninsula.

One of its most popular attractions is the re-created *Geraldine Street* in Ashe Hall in Denny Street. A buggy takes you back in time some 300 years, along a street peopled with life-like models in authentic dress engaged in the occupations of the era. *St John's Church*, in Castle Street, was built in 1870, and boasts a fine statue of St Brendan the Navigator, a native of the area. The *Dominican priory*, at Day Place, is a 19th-century revival of a 1243 foundation that succumbed to Cromwell's forces. In the grounds of the old *priory*, in Abbey Street, some 13 Earls of Desmond are buried and in the priory church there are superb works in stained glass by Michael Healy.

The *National Folk Theatre*, housed in the *Siamsa Tíre Theatre* in Tralee Town Park, stages a delightful re-creation of past Irish country life through music, song, dance and mime. Irish traditional music is also featured in many of the town's pubs.

## BACK TO NATURE

**2** *Castlegregory, Co Kerry*
Tucked away in the mountains near Castlegregory, **Gleann Ti An Easaigh/Glenteenassig Forest Park** is a feast for the naturalist. It lies a little over 13 miles (22km) west of Tralee on the **R560** to Castlegregory. Watch for signposting at Aughacasla and turn left into the mountains for 3 miles (5km). Alive with rushing streams and tiny lakes, the park is the habitat of many species of wildlife, as well as a refuge for a wide variety of birds. Mountain walks yield panoramic views of Tralee Bay and the western tip of the peninsula, and the picnic site is perfect for lunch.

*Visitors receive a warm welcome in Dingle's bars and restaurants*

*Continue southwest for 5 miles (8km), descending to Dingle town.*

### Dingle, Co Kerry

**4** County Kerry's chief port in the old days of Spanish trading, and a walled town in the Elizabethan era, Dingle town today is a busy little market, fishing and tourism centre with a boat-building industry right on the harbour. Although Dingle is in the heart of a district in which Irish is the everyday language, communication need present no problem, since conversations with visitors are held in English.

Dingle is ideal walking territory, its highlights being in a compact area of tiny streets that climb upward from the seafront. In addition to its sightseeing attractions, the town has several very good Irish goods shops, and there are boat rides out into the bay to see Dingle's resident dolphin (see For Children).

The **Old Presbytery** in Main Street has fascinating exhibits of historical photos and memorabilia from Dingle's colourful past. On the western edge

of town, the **Cearolann Craft Village** is a cluster of small cottages housing shops and workshops that sell silverware and jewellery crafts by a master silversmith, handcrafted leather goods, handmade Uilleann pipes, knitted goods, and the work of a cabinetmaker and weavers.

One of the town's most impressive collections of Irish-interest publications and records can be found in the front shop section of **An Café Liteartha** in Dykegate Street. For traditional music and song that stems from a long-time family tradition, look for the red-and-white pub on Bridge Street with the Irish name **UaFlaibeartaig**, which translates to O'Flaherty's. It is a warm, informal setting, as traditional as the music itself, its walls sporting the sort of haphazard collection of pictures, posters and other assorted items that have accumulated over the years, typical of many country pubs in Ireland. There is also music on summer nights at the **O Gairbhi Pub** and at **Garvey's Pub**, both on Strand Street, and at **Benner's Hotel** on Main Street.

*Drive due west on the **R559** for 6 miles (10km) through the village of Milltown to Ventry.*

## Ventry, Co Kerry

**5** According to legend – and a 15th-century manuscript now in the Bodleian Library at Oxford in England – Ventry beach was the scene of a fierce battle when the King of the World, Daire Doon, attempted to invade and conquer Ireland. He and his vassal monarchs, however, suffered a massive defeat at the hands of the King of Ireland, Fionn MacCumhaill (Finn MacCool), and his loyal Fianna band. The village nestles at the head of Ventry Harbour, with the slopes of Mount Eagle and Croagh Marhin as a backdrop. The black, beetle-like boats you will see upturned on the beach are *currachs*, the traditional canvas-covered canoe painted with tar that has been used by local fishermen in these waters for centuries.

Sheehy's Pottery, on the outskirts

*The beautiful but treacherous coastline of Slea Head, the westernmost point of Europe. Many ships have sunk off these dramatic cliffs*

of the village in an old, timber-ceilinged building that is almost a sightseeing attraction in itself, specialises in ceramic Celtic murals and plaques illustrating old Celtic myths. It also serves light meals of excellent home-cooked food.

*Continue southwest on the R559 for about 3 miles (5km) to Dunbeg.*

## Dunbeg, Co Kerry

**6** A relic of the Iron Age, Dunbeg Fort perches on a high promontory above Dingle Bay, its landward side surrounded by earthen trenches, and its 22-foot- (7m) thick wall riddled with an elaborate souterrain (inner passage). Originally, there was 'an inner enclosure, also with a souterrain, and a skilfully built inner house. Time has taken its toll on this strong defensive structure, for over the centuries portions have fallen down the steep cliffs to the sea.

*Cross the R559 to the Fahan archaeological grouping.*

## FOR CHILDREN

*Tralee, Co Kerry* Children seem to be born with a love of trains, and a very special train ride is provided by the narrow gauge **Tralee/Blennerville railway** that just runs along this portion of the long-abandoned Tralee/Dingle line. Less than a 5-mile (8km) round-trip journey, it is a thrill unmatched by any aboard the high-speed trains of this modern age.

**4** *Dingle, Co Kerry* What could be more fun for the younger ones than a boat ride out into Dingle Bay to watch Dingle's friendly dolphin, Fungi, playfully following the boats that leave from the town quays to ferry visitors out to his watery home, cavorting with scuba divers, and sometimes taking a flying leap over a small boat.

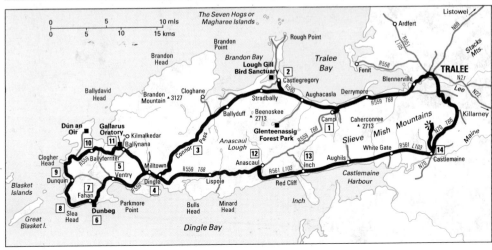

*Tralee, Co Kerry* Five-and-a-half miles (9km) northwest of Tralee via the Ballyheigue road (**R551**) is imposing **Ardfert Cathedral**, which dates from the 13th century. A niche in the building holds the 13th- or 14th-century effigy of a bishop unearthed here in 1830, and there is an ogham stone in the graveyard. The tiny village of **Fenit**, 8 miles (13km) west of Tralee via the **R558**, is thought to be the birthplace of St Brendan the Navigator (484–577), who may or may not have reached the shores of America long before the Vikings or Christopher Columbus.

**7** *Fahan, Co Kerry* About 3 miles (5km) above the main road (**R559**) at Fahan, an ancient road is lined with stone huts and other remains of ages past. The stone beehive huts, souterrains, standing and inscribed stones, earthen ringforts and two sculptured crosses, and two fortified headlands constitute Ireland's largest collection of antiquities.

Just past the village of Stradbally, you cross the deep Glennahoo Valley and begin the climb to the 1,500-foot (460m) summit of the Connor Pass, with spectacular views of valleys strewn with boulders and, about a mile from the summit, tiny **Pedlar's Lake**. The road upwards winds along the base of great cliffs. From the lay-by at the summit, there is a fine view of Dingle Bay and Dingle town to the south, with several small lakes in the deep valley to the left, and Brandon and Tralee bays to the north.

The drive along the **R559** from Ventry to Slea Head has a wide diversity of scenic pleasures, at times hugging the sides of sheer cliffs high above Dingle Bay, other stretches passing through stony fields reaching up sloping mountains.

The drive from **Red Cliff** to **Aughils** en route from Anascaul to Castlemaine via the **R561** (**L103**) follows a narrow, winding road set right into the sides of sheer, towering cliffs, with fantastic views south across Castlemaine Bay and north to the open sea and Dingle harbour. The views should be savoured from one of the tiny lay-bys along the way, since it is extremely dangerous to stop the car and block the road.

### Fahan, Co Kerry

**7** In farmyards (sometimes quite mucky) on the southern slopes of Mount Eagle across from Dunbeg, unmortared beehive cells, or *clochans*, (huts) are reminders of the prehistoric people who made their homes here and, quite possibly, built the promontory fort. It is a revelation to stoop down and enter one of these unique structures that are as water-tight today as when they were built.

*Continue west on the **R559** for 2 miles (3km) to Slea Head.*

### Slea Head, Co Kerry

**8** It is at the very tip of the Dingle Peninsula, from the high cliffs of Slea Head – the westernmost mainland point in Europe – that you get the most sweeping view of sheltered coves below and the Blasket Islands, sometimes called 'the last parish before America', across the water.

The **Great Blasket**, the largest of these seven offshore islands, was for many years home to a hardy band of islanders who inhabited the one small village. In 1953, when a living wage could no longer be wrested from fishing, its tiny population was moved to the mainland and given government grants for small farm holdings on the peninsula. A day trip to the islands is an experience of sheer tranquillity and scenic beauty that is unequalled anywhere else in Ireland. There are now plans afoot for the Irish Government to acquire the title to the Great Blasket and maintain it as an official National Historic Park, preserving the ruined village intact and developing activities that reflect the island's culture and traditions.

*Turn north, still on the **R559** for 2 miles (3km) to reach Dunquin.*

*Prehistoric beehive huts on the slopes of Mount Eagle near Fahan, one of several groups of archaeological remains in the area*

### Dunquin, Co Kerry

**9** Dunquin Pottery, on the road between Slea Head and Dunquin, is another of the excellent potteries on Dingle Peninsula. Its speciality is hand-thrown, ovenproof stoneware in shades of sand, browns and blues. Boats from Dunquin Harbour make intermittent trips out to the Blasket Islands (see Slea Head) during summer months, and often arrangements can be made with individual boatmen when there is no sailing scheduled.

*Follow the **R559** north, then east to Ballyferriter.*

### Ballyferriter, Co Kerry

**10** The Ballyferriter Heritage Centre, with its interesting 'Treasures of the Dingle Peninsula' exhibition, occupies the old school house in the centre of the village. Dingle's long history is illustrated by more than 200 photographs, artefacts and text.

The West Kerry Co-op office, just off Main Street, issues an excellent illustrated guidebook to the Dingle Peninsula, with great detail on its many antiquities. The Co-op began in 1968 in an effort to stem the outgoing tide of young people who could not be supported by the large areas of untillable ground. There was a great danger that the unique culture and heritage of the Gaelic-speaking region would wither and die, but through the Co-op members of the farming community were able to import a special deep-ploughing machine to break up the layer of iron-ore that lay just beneath the surface of their land

and turn it into productive acres. More than 12,000 acres (4,850 hectares) have been reclaimed, and the Co-op's activities have expanded to include upgrading tourist facilities, and administering the summer-school programme that enrols students of all ages to study Gaelic and live with the local families who use the language in their everyday lives.

Louis Mulcahy, a potter of international repute, operates a pottery studio/workshop on the outskirts of town, turning out many items finished with glazes developed in the workshop. Giant jugs and vases, unusual lamp bases and beautiful wall plaques, all marked by Louis's distinctive designs, supplement the more usual dinner- and cookware.

Two miles (3km) southwest of Ballyferriter, turn north on to an unclassified, signposted road to reach the site of the 16th-century fortress Dún an Óir, the so-called 'golden fort', built within an ancient promontory fort at Smerwick. The harbour here

was the disembarkation point for an expedition of Spanish and Irish, along with their families and other retinue, who arrived in the September of 1580 and constructed a fort to support the cause of the Catholic Irish against the Protestant English. Bombarded from land and sea by English forces, the fort capitulated but over 600 were slaughtered – men, women and children – once they were disarmed. Poet, Edmund Spenser (most famous for *The Faerie Queene*) and possibly Sir Walter Raleigh were participants in the battle, which came to be known as the 'massacre of Smerwick Harbour'. There is an excellent safe beach here.

*Follow the **R559** northeast for 2 miles (3km) and turn right at the signpost to Gallarus Oratory.*

*Glashabeg, near Ballydavid, is a centre of the curragh-building industry. The curragh's high prow enables it to ride the waves safely*

## RECOMMENDED WALKS

The entire Dingle Peninsula invites walks off the one main road that circles westward from Dingle town, and the **Dingle Peninsula Walking Route**, which will become part of **The Kerry Way**, is at present under development, with details available from the tourist office in Tralee.

**12** *Anascaul, Co Kerry* On the Dingle road west of Anascaul, park the car for a short, easy walk north along a signposted road that leads to lovely **Anascaul Lake**, set in a boulder-strewn hollow. Hardy walkers with two or three hours to spare can continue around the lake and strike out across the hills of the Beenoskee Mountains to Stradbally and Castlegregory.

### Gallarus Oratory, Co Kerry

**11** This marvellous example of early Irish architecture is perhaps the most impressive of the peninsula's antiquities. Built in an inverted boat shape, it has remained completely watertight for more than 1,000 years, its unmortared stones perfectly fitted. At the crossroads just above Gallarus, turn left for **Kilmalkedar**, a 12th-century ruined church a short distance away. In the church is the famous 'Alphabet Stone', a standing pillar carved with both Roman and ogham characters. The east window of this medieval church is known locally as 'the eye of the needle' through which one must squeeze to achieve salvation.

*Proceed via an unclassified road to Ballynana, turning southeast on to the R559 (T68) to reach Milltown and Dingle. Continue driving east for 10 miles (16km) on the R559 (T68) to Anascaul.*

### Anascaul, Co Kerry

**12** Look for the **South Pole Inn** as you enter the village. It is named for the former proprietor, Tom Crean, a member of the Scott expedition to the Antarctic. Beautiful **Anascaul Lake** (signposted) is well worth a short detour, time permitting.

*Heading south, then east on the R561 (L103), pass through Red Cliff to reach Inch.*

### Inch, Co Kerry

**13** The wide, 4-mile-long (6km) sandy beach on this spit at the head of **Castlemaine Harbour** is one of the best bathing beaches on the peninsula. The high dunes backing the beach have yielded archaeological evidence of ancient dwelling

*The Gallarus Oratory near Ballyferriter is one of the earliest churches in Ireland*

sites, including kitchen middens. During summer months, there is sometimes horseback riding on the firm sand and in the gentle surf. From the cliffside drive, west of the village, views out over the Iveragh Peninsula across the water are nothing short of spectacular.

*Continue east along the R561 (L103) for 12 miles (19km) to the little town of Castlemaine.*

### Castlemaine, Co Kerry

**14** In the town, immediately after turning left on to the Tralee road (N70), turn left again and look for the unclassified road signposted viewing park less than 1 mile (2km) further on. There is a viewpoint about 2½ miles (4km) along this road, with splendid views of Castlemaine Harbour and beyond the Laune Valley to Killarney. A second viewpoint, a short distance beyond the first, looks north to Tralee Bay, Tralee town, and the Stacks Mountains.

*Return to the N70 and drive north to reach Tralee.*

Tralee – Camp **10 (16)**
Camp – Castlegregory **6 (10)**
Castlegregory – Connor Pass **11 (18)**
Connor Pass – Dingle **5 (8)**
Dingle – Ventry **6 (10)**
Ventry – Dunbeg **3 (5)**
Dunbeg – Slea Head **2 (3)**
Slea Head – Dunquin **2 (3)**
Dunquin – Ballyferriter **6 (10)**
Ballyferriter – Gallarus Oratory **2 (3)**
Gallarus Oratory – Anascaul **17 (27)**
Anascaul – Inch **5 (8)**
Inch – Castlemaine **12 (19)**
Castlemaine – Tralee **10 (16)**

---

**SPECIAL TO ...**

*Tralee, Co Kerry* The **Rose of Tralee International Festival**, which is in full sway for six days and nights in late August, is a fierce, but fun, competition to see which of the beauties of Irish lineage from around the world best fits the time-honoured description '. . . lovely and fair as the rose of the summer'. This gathering differs from other such competitions, which usually amount to little more than beauty pageants that take themselves quite seriously. This is a festival of light-hearted fun and frolic that includes parades, pipe bands, street entertainment, inter-festival singing competitions for the Folk Festival of Ireland and, finally, the crowning of the Rose.

*A tour round the Muckross estate takes in the famous landscaped gardens and rock garden, views of the lakes and the ruins of Muckross Abbey. The gardens are Killarney's best-known tourist attraction*

---

ⓘ Town Hall, Main Street

*Take the **R562 (T67)** northwest for 13 miles (21km) to Killorglin.*

## Killorglin, Co Kerry

**1** Perched on hills above the River Laune, Killorglin is an ideal starting point for the Ring of Kerry drive, a 112-mile (180km) scenic drive with an ever-changing panorama of mountains, lakes, cliffs, sandy beaches and craggy offshore islands. The route skirts the edges of the Iveragh Peninsula to Kenmare, then circles back over the mountains via Moll's Gap and Ladies' View to Killarney. Make this a leisurely drive with an overnight stop in order to savour all the magnificent scenery along the way.

In mid-August, this rather quiet little town is abuzz with the three-day **Puck (Poc) Fair**. It dates from 1613, and things get off to a rousing start when a tremendous male (or puck) goat is crowned King of the Fair. In the somewhat rowdy atmosphere, pubs stay open around the clock, and every sort of street entertainment goes on non-stop. This is also a traditional gathering place for the country's travelling people, who come to engage in some hard-driving horse trading. Just how all this began is a matter of dispute: some say a goat bleated to alert a shepherd boy of approaching enemy forces and he, in turn, alerted the town about impending attack. Those of a more prosaic turn of mind say it dates back to one ill-fated fair when only one goat was put up for sale, while others say it goes back to the worship of Lug, a Celtic god.

*Turn southwest on to the **N70** for 8 miles (13km) to Glenbeigh.*

---

# KILLARNEY & THE RING OF KERRY

Killarney ● Killorglin ● Glenbeigh ● Cahirciveen
Waterville ● Sneem ● Kenmare ● Moll's Gap
Ladies' View ● Killarney

**A**n abundance of natural beauty has drawn visitors to Killarney and its lakes for centuries. The scenic network of Lough Leane, Muckross Lake and Upper Lake in a broad valley west of Killarney is the single most powerful magnet for visitors. It was a quiet little market town until the 18th century, when Arthur Young, a visiting Englishman, discovered its superb setting and spread the word abroad. Today, its narrow, congested streets can make for nerve-racking driving, but it is a perfect town for exploring on foot.

The 1860 *Franciscan Friary* in College Street is noted for the fine stained glass window above its main entrance. *St Mary's Church of Ireland church* at the foot of Main Street, built in Early English style, has a richly adorned interior, and *St Mary's Cathedral* in New Street is a splendid Gothic structure with interesting stained glass windows and a majestic, vaulted interior. The *Frank Lewis Gallery*, Bridewell Lane, shows landscapes of the Killarney area, portraits, and sculptures by local artists.

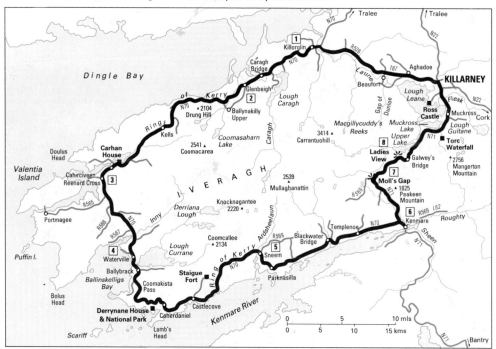

## FOR HISTORY BUFFS

*Killarney, Co Kerry* In ancient times, the **Hill of Aghadoe** just outside Killarney was the seat of the Celtic Archdruid. The **Annals of Inisfallen**, a chronicle of Irish history from the 11th to the 13th century, was recorded by dedicated monks on one of the Lower Lake's 30 islands.

## FOR CHILDREN

*Killarney, Co Kerry* Most children love being on the water, so what better way for them to see the Lakes of Killarney than aboard the watercoach *Lily of Killarney* that leaves the Ross Castle slipway several times daily to cruise the Lower Lake. They are sure to be fascinated by the mystical legends of the lake as related by the boatman as they glide past Inisfallen Island, O'Sullivan's Cascade, Tomies Mountain, Darby's Garden, the old copper mines, Library Point and many other points of interest.

## BACK TO NATURE

**3** *Cahirciveen, Co Kerry* If the seas are calm and you are a birdwatcher, make arrangements for a boatman in Cahirciveen to take you out to the two rocky islands that make up the **Skelligs**. Landing is difficult and not for the fainthearted, but the reward for climbing no fewer than 640 steps is the sight of thousands of puffins and other seabirds in residence in the protected bird sanctuary. The smaller of the two islands, Little Skellig, is a major breeding ground for gannets.

More accessible is **Puffin Island** which, as its name suggests, has breeding puffins, as well as Manx shearwaters. Boats go from Valentia Island.

## SCENIC ROUTES

From Waterville, the **N70** follows the coast, then lifts you some 700 feet (215m) above sea level at **Coomakista Pass**, with breathtaking views of the bay, the offshore **Skellig Islands**, and the coastline. It was on **Skellig Michael**, a massive rocky hulk that rises 700 feet (215m) above the sea, that a colony of early Christian monks built a retreat of stone beehive huts.

From Castlecove, the road turns inland through wild and gorgeous scenery before coming back to the coast at Sneem.

## Glenbeigh, Co Kerry

**2** On the main street of this small fishing village, known for its seafood, look for the bog village adjoining the Red Fox Inn. Bogs have always played an important role in Ireland, and this re-creation is an authentic depiction of the lives of the people centred around them.

*Follow the **N70** southwest for 17 miles (27km) to reach Cahirciveen.*

## Cahirciveen, Co Kerry

**3** The drive along the southern banks of Dingle Bay from Glenbeigh to this small town at the foot of the Bentee Mountain is one of island-dotted coastal scenery and fields studded with prehistoric stone ringfort ruins, with clear views of the Dingle Peninsula across the water. At Cahirciveen, **Valentia Island** comes into view. There is a ferry service during summer months, and it is accessible by car via a causeway further south at Portmagee. The island is noted for its superb scenery of cliffs, mountains, seascapes and vividly coloured subtropical flowers.

One mile (1.5km) northeast of Cahirciveen on the **N70**, **Carhan House**, the birthplace of Daniel O'Connell (1775), Ireland's beloved 'Liberator', stands in ruins.

*Drive 10 miles (16km) south on the **N70** to Waterville.*

## Waterville, Co Kerry

**4** Set on a strip of land that separates Ballinskelligs Bay from the island-sprinkled Lough Currane, this popular resort and angling centre is also internationally known for its superb golf- course. Mountains rise from the lake's eastern and southern shores, and on Church Island, there are ruins of a 12th-century church that was dedicated to the 6th-century St Fiann Cam.

*Continue south, then east on the **N70** for 22 miles (35km) to reach Sneem.*

## Sneem, Co Kerry

**5** On the drive east on the N70 from Waterville to Sneem, just east of Caherdaniel, is **Castlecove**, where, about 1½ miles (2km) north of the road you will see Staigue Fort, one of the country's best preserved Iron Age stone forts. The circular stone walls, 13 feet (4m) wide and 18 feet (5.5m) high, have held over the centuries without the benefit of mortar, and along their interior are several flights of stairs in near perfect condition.

Just beyond the **Coomakista Pass** on the N70, about 1 mile (1.5km) beyond Caherdaniel on the

---

*Jarvey rides are a popular and relaxed way of seeing the sights in the peaceful market town of Killarney*

*As the road winds through Moll's Gap it provides good views of the rugged mountain scenery*

Derrynane road, is **Derrynane House and National Park.** This is where 'The Liberator', Daniel O'Connell, lived for most of his political life, and the house is now maintained as a museum containing all sorts of O'Connell memorabilia.

The National Park covers some 320 acres (130 hectares), incorporating semi-tropical plants and coastal trees and shrubs, as well as fine coastal scenery. There is a well-marked nature trail, and sea bathing is accessible to visitors.

The tidy, picturesque little town of Sneem, situated where the Ardsheelaun river estuary joins Kenmare river, is a popular angling centre for brown trout and salmon, and its fine sandy beaches provide safe swimming. George Bernard Shaw wrote part of his play *St Joan* here. It is also the last resting place of Father Michael Walsh, who was parish priest in the area for 38 years in the 1800s and is immortalised as 'Father O'Flynn' in a well-known Irish ballad.

Two miles (3km) to the south in **Parknasilla,** the elegant **Great Southern Hotel** is famed for its rock gardens and colourful sub-tropical blooms.

*Continue east on the **N70** for 17 miles (27km) to Kenmare.*

## Kenmare, Co Kerry

**6** The drive from Sneem along the banks of the Kenmare river has lovely views of the Caha and Slieve Miskish mountains on the opposite shore. Kenmare faces the broad Kenmare river estuary, with impressive mountains at its back.

Known as *Ceann Mara* ('Head of the Sea') by the ancients, today it is a lively resort noted for its fine salmon, brown trout and sea fishing; safe swimming; local walks and climbs; homespun woollen industry; and lace-making. (See also Tour 6.)

*Turn north onto the **N71** to reach Moll's Gap.*

## Moll's Gap, Co Kerry

**7** The drive north to Moll's Gap is one of rugged mountains and stone-strewn valleys. The viewing point at this gap affords sweeping views of Macgillycuddy's Reeks and of Ireland's highest mountain, 3,414-foot (1,040m) Carrantuohill. The restaurant and craft shop make this a good refreshment stop.

### RECOMMENDED WALKS

*Killarney, Co Kerry* Just across the road from the Cathedral in Killarney, the wooded walks of Knockreer estate offer a welcome retreat from congested town streets. A short walk brings you to **Knockreer House,** with marvellous exhibits of the flora, fauna and wildlife of the area. A longer walk takes you to the ruins of **Ross Castle** (about 1½ miles (2.5km) from the town centre) on a long peninsula out into the Lower Lake. Built in the 14th century, it was a prominent fortification during the Cromwellian wars in the 1600s. You can hire a boat here to begin your tour of the lakes.

An exhilarating walk is that over the **Gap of Dunloe,** for which you should allow a minimum of three hours.

**The Kerry Way,** a splendid walk of approximately 36½ miles (60km), has been laid out for dedicated walkers. It begins at Killarney National Park and extends to Glenbeigh, and further extensions are in the planning stage. The Tourist Office in Killarney can furnish full details.

Follow the **N71** northeast for 3 miles (5km) to Ladies' View.

### Ladies' View, Co Kerry

**8** This viewing point on a mountainside overlooks the broad valley that holds the lakes. Queen Victoria and her ladies-in-waiting so enthused about this view that it was promptly named in their honour.

Nine miles (14.5km) north on the return to Killarney, the well-preserved ruins of Muckross Abbey are situated. The abbey dates from 1448 and was built on the site of an earlier religious establishment. Four miles (6km) south off the N71, about a 10-minute walk from the abbey, Elizabethan-style Muckross House is surrounded by landscaped gardens that slope down to the lake. Built by a wealthy Kerry MP in 1843, it was sold to Americans in 1911, and presented as a gift to the Irish people in 1932. The first two floors are furnished in the manner of the great houses of Ireland, while its upper floors hold fascinating exhibits of maps, prints and other documents, as well as a small wildlife and bird collection. In the basement there is a folk museum with a country pub, printshop, dairy, carpentry shop and weaving shop.

Muckross House was built in the 19th century in the Elizabethan style. It now houses a craft centre and exhibitions of furniture, old maps and prints, farm machinery and a variety of other artefacts

Craftspeople are at work in some, and you can purchase their products in the gift shop. A light, airy tea-shop is just off the courtyard.

About 1 mile (1.5km) before Muckross House, a signpost on the N71 directs you to a scenic footpath up a mountain slope to the 60-foot (18m) Torc Waterfall in a beautiful wooded area. Continue upwards to the top of the falls for magnificent views.

Continue for 11 miles (18km) northeast on the **N71** to Killarney.

Killarney – Killorglin **13 (21)**
Killorglin – Glenbeigh **8 (13)**
Glenbeigh – Cahirciveen **17 (27)**
Cahirciveen – Waterville **10 (16)**
Waterville – Sneem **22 (35)**
Sneem – Kenmare **17 (27)**
Kenmare – Moll's Gap **6 (10)**
Moll's Gap – Ladies' View **3 (5)**
Ladies' View – Killarney **11 (18)**

---

### SPECIAL TO...

*Killarney, Co Kerry*
**Pan-Celtic Week** in Killarney in mid-May is a gathering of Celts from six countries to celebrate and preserve their ancient ties. Activities include sports competitions, workshops, concerts, pipe band competitions, informal sessions, dancing, and a marvellous **Cornish Pen Gwyn** torchlight procession featuring ancient dance rhythms.

*The islands in the sheltered harbour of the little fishing port of Glengarriff are a good place to spot seals basking in the sun*

# KENMARE & THE BEARA PENINSULA

Kenmare ● Glengarriff ● Adrigole ● Castletownbere
Allihies ● Eyeries ● Ardgroom ● Kenmare

i Kenmare (June to September)

*Drive south for 18 miles (29km) on the **N71** to reach Glengarriff.*

## Glengarriff, Co Cork

**1** The 18-mile (29km) drive from Kenmare to Glengarriff (Rugged Glen) is known as the 'Tunnel Road'. Two tunnels, one the longest in Ireland, bore through the Caha Mountains, and the road alternately climbs mountain heights and dips into deep valleys. The sky in these parts seems to expand to the edges of eternity, and the play of light and shadow from ever-shifting clouds is nothing short of spectacular.

Lying in the heart of a secluded valley surrounded by mountains, Glengarriff's sheltered position nurtures luxuriant Mediterranean flowers and plants such as fuchsia and arbutus. Its harbour is dotted with wooded islands, on one of which – **Garinish Island** – are the world-famous Italian gardens, laid out between 1910 and 1913 by John Annan Bryce and Harold Peto. The lovely little island was a favourite of George Bernard Shaw, who came here to write much of his *St Joan*.

Only the strongest-willed visitor will be able to resist the entreaties of the bold boatmen who line the main street hawking a trip to the gardens; those who pass on by will be the poorer for it.

Glengarriff is also one of the few places in the country that preserves remnants of ancient mixed forests, best seen at **Glengarriff Forest Park**, on the northern edge of the village. Here there are oak, elm, pine, yew, mountain ash, rowan and holly trees that covered much of Ireland in ancient days.

The attractive town of Kenmare, at the head of Kenmare Bay, was founded by Sir William Petty in 1670, who set up iron works, lead mines and other industries. Today, it is a thriving market town and tourist centre. It makes an excellent base for exploring the Iveragh and Beara peninsulas. Its famous school of needlepoint and lace-making, founded in 1861, is in the *Convent of the Poor Clares*, next to the Catholic church opposite the market house. One of Ireland's most impressive stone circles, the *Druid's Circle*, with 15 standing stones round a dolmen of three uprights and a large capstone, is on the left bank of the River Finnehy between the bridge and an area known as The Shrubberies, site of an ancient abbey of which no traces remain. There is excellent swimming and surfing at the pier, signposted from the Glengarriff road (*N71*). (See also Tour 5.)

Along with the boatmen hawking the trip to Garinish Island, the main street is lined with shops offering an extensive range of Irish crafts at bargain prices. Just off the main

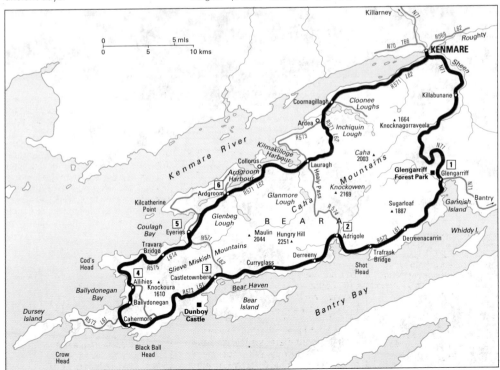

*The formal Italian gardens on Garinish Island were laid out between 1910 and 1913. A wide variety of plants flourish in the mild subtropical climate*

street, **Donal Houlihan's Handcraft Shop** features woollens and tweeds that you can see being woven on the premises.

Glengarriff lies at the head of the Beara Peninsula, a 30-mile (48km) long, mountainous finger of land between Bantry Bay and the Kenmare river. It is bisected by the Cork/Kerry county border running along the Caha mountain range that runs down the centre of the peninsula. A drive around this wild, sparsely populated peninsula constitutes the remainder of this tour.

*Drive about 12 miles (19km) southwest on the R572 (L61) to Adrigole.*

**FOR HISTORY BUFFS**

*Kenmare, Co Kerry* Cross the bridge over the River Finnehy at Kenmare to find an impressive stone circle and dolmen. There are 15 stones in the circle, which measures about 50 feet (15m) across. In its centre is the dolmen, a megalithic tomb where upright stones support a large, flat capstone.

### Adrigole, Co Cork

**2** From Glengarriff, the road follows the shoreline of Bantry Bay, winding along the rocky coastal strip at the foot of the Caha Mountains, with 1,887-foot (575m) **Sugarloaf Mountain** on the right. At Adrigole Bridge, the spectacular **Healy Pass** crosses the mountains and is an alternative (and shorter) route to Kenmare and Killarney.

Some 3 miles (5km) west of Adrigole, **Hungry Hill**, highest of the Caha range, rises 2,251 feet (686m), with a rocky shelf halfway up its face on which are two lakes that feed a 700-foot (214m) cascade into the valley below – especially spectacular after rain. The peak was the source of the title for Daphne du Maurier's novel, *Hungry Hill*.

*Continue southwest for another 9 miles (14km) on the R572 (L61) to Castletownbere.*

## Castletownbere, Co Cork

**3** Sheltered by the elongated Bere (Bear) Island just offshore, Castletownbere, now a fishing port, was once a British naval base. There is a regular ferry service out to the island, where some forts still remain, manned from time to time by Irish forces. On a hillside near the old waterworks, look for a group of **boulder burials** and a fine **stone circle**, the latter on the western side of the hill.

Less than 2 miles (3km) west of town, facing Bere Island, are the remains of 16th-century **Dunboy Castle**, in spacious grounds overlooking the inlet. This star-shaped fort was the stronghold of O'Sullivan Bere, the last Irish leader to hold out with Spanish allies against British forces led by Sir George Carew in 1602. After a long siege, during which the garrison refused to surrender until the walls were completely shattered, the fort was all but destroyed. The ruins have been excavated for easy exploration.

The grandiose ruined mansion sited between the castle and Castletownbere was the home of the Puxley family, copper-mining moguls whose family and mining history form the basis of Daphne du Maurier's novel *Hungry Hill*.

Fifteen miles (24km) further west, Ireland's only cable-car connects **Dursey Island** with the mainland. The beautiful, long, mountainous island is rimmed by high cliffs and is the site of a gannetry.

*Continue southwest on the **R572 (L61)** to its junction with the **R575 (L61A)**, which turns north to Allihies, a total of 12 miles (19km).*

*The Healy Pass, 1,084 feet (330m) at its highest point, provides good views of the mountains of the Beara Peninsula*

### FOR CHILDREN

**1** *Glengarriff, Co Cork*
A delightful bonus for children on the short boat ride from Glengarriff Pier to Garinish Island, about 1 mile (1.5km) offshore in Bantry Bay, is the sight of seals cavorting through the waters. The island's beautiful Italian gardens are a riot of colour in season, with subtropical plants in gorgeous bloom. Turn the children loose to wander along the woodland pathways, through the formal gardens, and down to the shores of the bay, or to explore the Grecian temple and old Martello Tower.

### RECOMMENDED WALKS

*Kenmare, Co Kerry* Walk out along the Glengarriff road **(N71)** from Kenmare and turn right at the signpost for the pier. Try to go when the tide is in as the views of the Kenmare river are at their most impressive then. The river, with its backdrop of surrounding mountains and drifts of graceful swans, presents a view of tranquillity and natural beauty that provides ample reward for the short walk.

**1** *Glengarriff, Co Cork*
Scenic walks in Glengarriff include the **Blue Pool**, via a pathway west of the post office; **Lady Bantry's Lookout**, 2 miles (3km) southwest of the village on the Castletownbere road, returning by Shrove Hill viewpoint; or continue past Lady Bantry's Lookout to **Eagle's Nest**, and from there to **Biddy's Cove** on the shores of the bay.

### SCENIC ROUTES

At Adrigole Bridge, turn right for the Healy Pass road. Begun during the famine, the road, after years of stopping and starting, and a high death-rate during its construction, was completed in 1931 and named for Tim Healy, the first governor-general of the Irish Free State when it became a dominion in 1922. This spectacular drive, of about 10 miles (16km), climbs right across the spine of the Caha mountain range and across the Cork/Kerry border, with magnificent views of **Glanmore Lough**, the forests of **Tousist, Kenmare Bay** and **Macgillycuddy's Reeks**. There is a viewing point and crucifixion shrine at the top.

---

### BACK TO NATURE

**6** *Ardgroom, Co Cork* About 8 miles (13km) southwest of Kenmare on the **R571**, signposts point into a valley of exceptional botanical interest. **Inchiquin Lough**, one of the chain known as the Cloonee loughs, has marvellous views and a lovely waterfall. In the early summer, the large-flowered butterwort *(Pinguicula grandiflora)* flowers freely, and across the lake, **Uragh Wood** holds ancient oakwoods, which have all but disappeared from Ireland, along with saxifrages, Irish spurge, strawberry tree and rhododendrons. For the best view of the lake, waterfall and Uragh Wood, follow the tarred road along the edge of Inchiquin Lough.

### SPECIAL TO...

*Kenmare, Co Kerry* As you might expect from this watery area, the seafood is outstanding. From local lakes, rivers and surf come bass, conger, pollock, ray, mullet and mackerel. These are, of course, supplemented by deep-sea fish brought in by fishermen who ply these waters for a livelihood. The elegant, late-Victorian style Park Hotel, whose cuisine has earned it a Michelin star, specialises in the best local seafood. With lovely views of the estuary and mountains, the hotel has a garden setting. The Purple Heather Bistro is an old-fashioned pub/restaurant that also serves superb seafood in a casual setting.

*The view towards Allihies, an unspoilt village with good beaches. The area was originally a rich copper-mining district*

### Allihies, Co Cork

**4** The road from Castletownbere continues southwest to **Black Ball Head** before turning northwest to reach Allihies through a gap in the hills. This was once a rich copper-mining centre that provided the basis for the Puxley family fortunes. The 19th century was their most prosperous period, although some work continued right up to 1962. There are picturesque ruins on the scarred hillsides, but they should be explored with extreme caution, since the old workings, with unguarded shafts, can be very dangerous.

Seascapes from the hills are breathtaking, the strand is safe for swimming, and just north of the village there is an old mass rock.

*Follow the **R575 (L61A)** northeast for about 10 miles (16km) to Eyeries.*

### Eyeries, Co Cork

**5** From Allihies, the road leads northeast along the Kenmare river through rugged scenery to the little village of Eyeries, set back from the sea on a pretty bay.

A little to the north, at **Ballycrovane**, there is an inscribed **ogham pillar stone** thought to be the tallest in western Europe, at more than 17½

feet (5.18m) high. In general, ogham stones served as gravestones and the signs on them record the buried person's name.

*Continue northeast on the **R571 (L62)** for 14 miles (23km) to Ardgroom.*

### Ardgroom, Co Cork

**6** Just beyond the little village of Ardgroom, you cross into Kerry, where there is yet another fine **stone circle** in **Canfie**, on the Lauragh road.

**Lauragh**, at the northern end of the Healy Pass, has a scenic ridge walk along a horseshoe of peaks surrounding the valley in which the village stands. Nearby is almost totally enclosed Kilmakilloge harbour, where boats can be hired to sail the safe harbour waters. A little beyond Lauragh, look for signposts directing you inland to Cloonee and Inchiquin loughs, both worth a detour. Rejoining the main road, the R571 (L62), the drive into Kenmare follows the shores of Kenmare Bay, with scenic views along one of the most striking stretches of the journey.

*Take the **R571 (L62)** for 21 miles (34km) back to Kenmare.*

Kenmare – Glengarriff **18 (29)**
Glengarriff – Adrigole **12 (19)**
Adrigole – Castletownbere **9 (14)**
Castletownbere – Allihies **12 (19)**
Allihies – Eyeries **10 (16)**
Eyeries – Ardgroom **14 (23)**
Ardgroom – Kenmare **21 (34)**

*A street artist attracts a crowd in Cork, where street theatre and entertainment are among its many attractions. Cork is the cultural capital of Ireland, having many galleries, museums and old buildings, and is best explored on foot*

# ISLAND CITY, MAGIC STONE

Cork ● Blarney ● Kanturk ● Mallow ● Mitchelstown
Cahir ● The Vee ● Lismore ● Youghal ● Cork

[i] Tourist House, Grand Parade

*Cross Patrick Street bridge and turn left for the signposted 6-mile (10km) drive northwest on the R617 (L69) to reach Blarney.*

## Blarney, Co Cork

**1** The well-preserved ruins of Blarney Castle, built in 1446, draw visitors not for their history, but rather for the magical powers attributed to the famous stone embedded in its parapet wall. The legend of its powers arose from Queen Elizabeth I's frustration in dealing with Cormac MacCarthy, Lord of Blarney, and his smiling flattery that veiled wiliness with eloquence. Her declaration that 'This is nothing but Blarney – what he says, he never means!' added a new word to the English language and probably gave rise to the legend of the 'gift of eloquence' associated with the stone. Kissing the magical stone, however, involves climbing 120 steep steps to lie on your back and hang over an open space.

About 200 yards (180m) from the castle is the superb Scottish baronial mansion, **Blarney Castle House**, with fine 18th-century gardens. The house has been beautifully restored and provides an ideal setting for its elegant furnishings.

**Blarney woollen mills** are also worth a visit.

*Leave Blarney on the R617 (L69) and a few miles from the village turn right on to the R579 (L9) for the 30-mile (48km) drive to Kanturk.*

Spreading out along a long valley between hills to the north and south, Cork had its beginning in the 6th or 7th century, when St Finbar established a monastery here on a small island surrounded by marshes. *St Finbar's Cathedral* on Bishop's Street may mark the site, although the present structure dates from about 1870.

*Crawford Art Gallery* on Emmet Place contains exhibits by modern Irish artists and an interesting collection of classical casts from the Vatican Galleries. Nearby *Lavitt's Quay Gallery* shows paintings, sculpture, ceramics and batiks. The *Protestant church* is noted for its red-and-white 'pepper-pot' steeple. The clocks set in its four sides are known far and wide as the 'four-faced liar', since no two of them ever show the same time, and it holds the famed 'Bells of Shandon'. The *City Hall*, on Albert Quay, is the setting for many of Cork's festivals and other special events. Theatre, musical reviews, concerts and other entertainments are presented at the *Cork Opera House*, and the *Everyman Theatre* on MacCurtain Street is the venue for productions by local, national and international theatre companies. (See also Tour 8.)

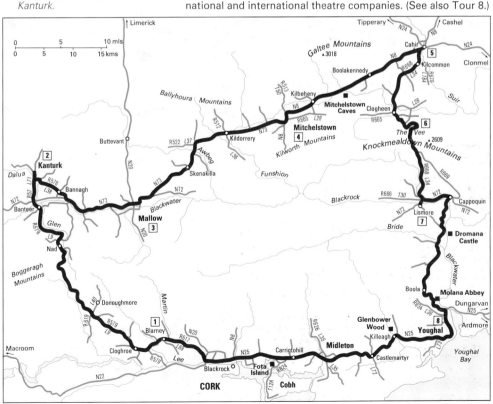

## FOR HISTORY BUFFS

*Cork, Co Cork* Six miles (10km) east of Cork city on the main Cork–Cobh road, the **R624 (T12A), Fota Island** is a 790-acre (320-hectare) estate now housing **Fota Island House, Arboretum and Wildlife Park**. The impressive Regency manor house was built in the 1820s, when the arboretum was also begun. Its elegantly proportioned rooms have period wallpapers, fine woodwork, moulded ceilings, 18th- and 19th-century furnishings, and exhibitions of outstanding Irish landscape paintings.

## FOR CHILDREN

*Cork, Co Cork* The **Fota Island Wildlife Park** is a child's paradise, inhabited by an engaging animal population that includes zebras, cheetahs, kangaroos, giraffes, ostriches, antelopes, gibbons and monkeys, as well as rare and endangered species. There are pools for flamingos and penguins, and swans float serenely on the lake. A tour train is great fun, and there is a children's corner and playground. Round off the day at one of the picnic spots.

## RECOMMENDED WALK

*Cork, Co Cork* There is a fine river walk in Cork between rows of old trees, with seats and rustic shelters sprinkled along the way. The river widens into Cork harbour, and on the opposite bank fine townhouses climb up the hills of the Montenotte and Tivoli residential sections. The small fishing village suburb of Blackrock is at the end of the Marina, with **Blackrock Castle** on a little promontory jutting out into the Lee.

## SPECIAL TO...

*Cork, Co Cork* The high-spirited **International Jazz Festival** in October attracts some of the world's most outstanding musicians, with concerts all around the town, as well as impromptu jam sessions breaking out in pubs, B&B drawing rooms, and wherever two jazz devotees happen to meet.

The **Cork Film Festival** in late September or early October enjoys a worldwide reputation as a showcase for independent film-makers.

*Mitchelstown Caves are the largest cave system in Ireland, and extend for miles. The large caverns were created by the action of water on the rock*

### Kanturk, Co Cork

**2** One mile (1.5km) south of town, unfinished **Kanturk Castle** was begun in 1609 by Irish chieftain MacDonagh MacCarthy, who planned it as the largest mansion in Ireland, following the Anglo-Norman design of a large quadrangle with four-storey towers at each corner. Alarmed at its size and strength, the English Privy Council ordered work to cease, declaring it was 'much too large for a subject'. The roofless, stout walls and towers have survived in remarkable condition.

*Drive southeast on the **R576 (L38)** to its junction with the **N72**, then turn east for 9 miles (14km) to reach Mallow.*

### Mallow, Co Cork

**3** Set on the Blackwater river, Mallow was a popular spa town during the 18th and early 19th centuries; its lively social life prompted the famous song, *The Rakes of Mallow*. The fine, **fortified house** built in the 16th century to replace 12th-century Mallow Castle, itself burned in 1689 on the orders of James II, now stands in fairly complete ruins in its own park by the river crossing.

About 9 miles (14km) north of Mallow, via the N20, the little town of **Buttevant** saw the world's first steeplechase in 1752, run between its church steeple and the one in Doneraile.

On the outskirts of town are the remains of **Ballybeg**, an **Augustinian Canons' Regular House**, enclosed by low stone walls, that dates back to 1237. The ruins include a dovecot with ranks of stone nesting boxes inside.

*Take the **N73** northeast for 21 miles (34km) to Mitchelstown.*

### Mitchelstown, Co Cork

**4** This is a tidy, attractive landlord-planned town founded in the early 19th century. Ten miles (16km) northeast of town via the N8, the signposted **Mitchelstown Caves** are an underground wonderland of linked passages and high-ceilinged chambers, including the biggest chamber in the British Isles. The Old Caves were used as a refuge for a 16th-century Earl of Desmond, with a price on his head. There are escorted tours through 2 miles (3km) of this fantastic netherworld, with its fine stalactite formations.

*Follow the **N8** for 18 miles (29km) northeast to Cahir.*

### Cahir, Co Tipperary

**5** Cahir Castle occupies a small islet in the River Suir, a natural site for fortifications as far back as the 3rd century. The present castle was built in the 13th century by the de Berminghams and was held by the Anglo-Norman Butlers until 1599, when the Earl of Essex captured it after a three-day siege that left gaping breaches in the east walls. Oliver Cromwell made a fierce show of force before the walls in 1650 and sent in surrender terms. Historians differ as to whether the garrison accepted the terms immediately or held out until they saw the heavy ordnance ranged against them. They did, however, surrender before the walls were battered again, and the castle thus remained in sound condition. It has been restored almost to its original condition, and there is an excellent audio-visual show in the 1840 courtyard cottage. (See also Tour 10.)

*Head south on the **R668 (L34)** through the village of Clogheen to begin The Vee mountain pass road en route to Lismore.*

*Blarney Castle is famous for the Blarney Stone. The legend goes that kissing the stone gives you the gift of the Blarney. However, you have to climb 120 steps up to it first*

### The Vee, Co Tipperary and Waterford

**6** The viewing points along this drive through a gap in the Knockmealdown Mountains provide spectacular panoramic views of Killballyboy Wood, Boernagore Wood, the Galtee Mountains, the Golden Vale of Tipperary, Bay Lough and the Comeragh mountain range. (See also Tour 10.)

*Continue south on the R668 (L34) for 8 miles (13km) to Lismore.*

### Lismore, Co Waterford

**7** This historic little town, site of an ancient monastic centre of learning, is beautifully situated on the banks of the Blackwater river. Its most outstanding sightseeing attractions are **Lismore Castle** whose gardens are open to the public, the Protestant cathedral, with grave slabs from the 9th and 11th centuries, and the modern Romanesque-style Catholic cathedral. (See also Tour 10.)

*Take the N72 east for 4 miles (6km) to the bridge on the outskirts of Cappoquin and turn right on to an unclassified road to a T-junction. Turn right on to the road signposted Youghal that follows the River Blackwater south to the sea, then turn right on to the N25 south for the short drive into Youghal.*

### SCENIC ROUTES

**7** *Lismore, Co Waterford*
About 1 mile (1.5km) from the Cappoquin bridge, the scenic 10-mile (16km) route to Youghal follows the Blackwater river, with deeply wooded stretches as well as superb views of the broad river and the opposite banks. Great houses of the 19th century and earlier are dotted along the route, and about 2 miles (3km) south of Cappoquin, the large house high above the east bank is the remodelled wing of ancient **Dromana Castle**, where traces of the old gardens sloping down to the river can still be seen.

**8** *Youghal, Co Cork* About
5 miles (8km) west of
Youghal on the **N25**, the
entrance to **Glenbower
Wood** is at the Thatch Inn in
Killeagh village. Its nature trail
is a 1½ mile (3km) loop that
can be walked in about half
an hour, or fully savoured for
an hour or two. The wood is
set in a glen through which
the River Dissour rushes, and
at one point an earthen dam
was built to power the village
corn mill, forming a lovely
lake. Native trees include
hazel (considered to have
magical powers to ward off
evil), sessile oak, alder, scrub
oak, holly, birch and rowan.
Tree plantations are mostly
Norway spruce, Western
hemlock and Sitka spruce.
The profusion of ferns include
hard fern, bracken fern, hart's
tongue and the male shield
fern. An ideal spot for a
picnic.

### Youghal, Co Cork

**8** This picturesque fishing harbour
and seaside resort is filled with
mementoes of its past. Sir Walter
Raleigh lived here and legend has it
that this is where he first smoked
tobacco from the New World and
planted the first potato in Irish soil.
**Myrtle Grove**, his Elizabethan house,
is at the top of Nelson Place, but it is
still a private residence and not open
to the public.

A Tourist Trail booklet available
from the Tourist Office details a
signposted walking tour of the town,
which includes the historic **Clock
Tower** in the town centre that was
erected in 1771 as a gaol and now
holds an art gallery and museum
featuring the works of local artists,
ancient town charters and Sir Walter
Raleigh memorabilia. A short distance
away there are fragments of the old
town walls, constructed in 1275 and
added to up until 1603. During
summer months there are harbour
and river cruises as well as deep-sea
fishing charters.

As the Blackwater river broadens
near its entrance to the sea north of
Youghal, look for the extensive ruins
of 13th-century **Molana Abbey**,
situated on what was once an islet.
Although rather overgrown, the site

*Lismore's Catholic cathedral,
dedicated to St Carthach, is a
modern building in the
Romanesque style. It has a
beautiful bell-tower and altar*

holds ruins of a church, cloisters and
conventual buildings, as well as what
is believed to be the burial place of the
Norman knight, Raymond le Gros.

Eight miles (13km) east of Youghal,
via a signposted turnoff from the **N25**,
the pretty little seaside village of
**Ardmore** grew from a 7th-century
settlement founded by St Declan and
has a fine group of ecclesiastical
remains, including one of the most
perfectly preserved round towers in
Ireland. There are also bracing cliff
walks along the sea's edge.

*i* Market House, Market Square

*Follow the **N25** west for 28 miles
(45km) to return to Cork.*

Cork – Blarney **6 (10)**
Blarney – Kanturk **30 (48)**
Kanturk – Mallow **13 (21)**
Mallow – Mitchelstown **21 (34)**
Mitchelstown – Cahir **18 (29)**
Cahir – The Vee **14 (23)**
The Vee – Lismore **8 (13)**
Lismore – Youghal **21 (34)**
Youghal – Cork **28 (45)**

*St Finbar's Hermitage at Gougane Barra on an island in the lake is commemorated by a tiny chapel built in 1901 in the Romanesque style*

[i] Tourist House, Grand Parade

*Take the **R600 (L42)** south for 16 miles (26km) to Kinsale.*

### Kinsale, Co Cork

**1** The fishing and boating village of Kinsale has figured prominently in Ireland's history since it received its charter in 1334. A decisive British victory here in 1601 led to a mass exodus of Irish royalty known as the 'Flight of the Earls'.

Twelfth-century **St Multose Church** displays the old town stocks, and there are ruins of a 12th-century **Carmelite friary** and 15th-century **Desmond Castle**. The atmospheric **Seanachie Pub** on Market Street has good traditional music, and **The Spaniard** is a favourite haunt of international yachtsmen and local fishermen.

Near **Summer Cove**, there are extensive, well-preserved remains of **Charles Fort**, built around 1677, with spectacular views of Kinsale harbour.

Seven miles (11km) south via the R600 (L42) and R604 is the **Old Head of Kinsale**, where a ruined clifftop castle overlooks the spot where the *Lusitania* was sunk in 1915 by a German submarine.

*Continue on the **R600 (L42)** for 22 miles (35km) southwest to Clonakilty.*

*The pretty port of Kinsale is built around a wide harbour, and has steep narrow streets. It is popular with yachtsmen and sea anglers alike*

# CORK'S COASTAL VILLAGES

**Cork ● Kinsale ● Clonakilty ● Rosscarbery ● Leap Dunmanway ● Gougane Barra ● Macroom ● Cork**

Its great age and its location in a long, marshy valley have fashioned Cork City into what a native son once aptly described as 'an intimate higgledy-piggledy assemblage of steps, slopes, steeples and bridges'. At the junction of Grand Parade and South Mall, *The National Monument* commemorates Irish rebels in the 1798 and 1867 uprisings, and at the foot of Patrick Bridge, the Father Matthew statue depicts the beloved temperance leader.

The lively *English Market* was established in 1610, although the present building was erected in 1782. Running parallel to the Western Road is the *Mardyke*, a mile-long (1.5km) tree-shaded walk bordered by *Fitzgerald Park*, the site of interesting modern Irish sculptures, and the *Cork Museum*, which traces the city's history from prehistoric times to the present. The old *Butter Exchange* near St Anne's Church now houses the *Shandon Craft Centre*, while the *Triskel Arts Centre* in Tobin Street presents contemporary theatre, films and music. (See also Tour 7.)

### FOR HISTORY BUFFS

**1** *Kinsale, Co Cork* When Don Juan d'Aguila arrived in Kinsale from Spain in 1601 with a large force to assist the Irish rebels against the English forces, an Irish victory seemed certain, even though the English Lord Deputy, Mountjoy, threw some 12,000 soldiers into the siege of the town. Irish chieftains O'Donnell and O'Neill marched their troops down from the north to mount a rear offensive against the English. This might well have succeeded had not word reached Mountjoy of their strategy, enabling him to successfully rout both Irish and Spanish. South of the town the remains of **King James Fort** (or **Old Fort**), which housed the Spanish, can be visited.

## Clonakilty, Co Cork

**2** Ten miles (16km) from Kinsale, on the Clonakilty road, **Timoleague Castle Gardens** were laid out more than one and a half centuries ago. **Timoleague Abbey** is a well-preserved ruined Franciscan friary, which in its day was an important religious centre.

At Clonakilty, castles dot the shores of the bay, the **Catholic church** is a fine example of Gothic architecture, and the **West Cork Regional Museum** displays archaeological relics and town corporation minute books going back to 1675, along with memorabilia of Irish resistance leader, Michael Collins. The **Michael Collins Birthplace** is about 2 miles (3km) west at Woodfield.

Two miles (3km) south of town, **Inchydoney**, a promontory running into Clonakilty Bay, has a fine beach, one of many in this area.

*Continue southwest on the **N71** for 8 miles (13km) to Rosscarbery.*

## Rosscarbery, Co Cork

**3** At the head of Rosscarbery Bay, this picturesque little town was the site of a medieval **Benedictine monastery** in the 6th century, founded by St Fachtna, and was famous for its school. A few remains of its foundation can be seen near the **Church of Ireland church** which stands on the site of an ancient cathedral.

One mile (1.5km) east of town are the ruins of **Benduff Castle**, and a little further on, the beautiful demesne of **Castlefreke**. Two miles (3km) west of town, the fine **Drombeg stone circle** can be seen from the Glandore road R597 (L191), and nearby is **Fulacht Fiadh stone trough**, an ancient Celtic cooking pot in which water was brought to the boil with heated stones.

*Take the **N71** west for 5 miles (8km) to Leap.*

## Leap, Co Cork

**4** This pretty little village sits at the head of a narrow inlet where the River Leap (pronounced 'lep') enters Glandore harbour. Stop in at the **Leap Inn** on the main street to experience an authentic Irish country inn that has been run by the same family for generations and has a cosy bar and lounge enlivened by the colourful conversation of locals and a dining-room that serves good, solid traditional Irish favourites.

Climb the hill above the village for beautiful harbour views, and drive to nearby **Unionhall** on a scenic road that follows the harbour as it widens to enter the sea.

*Take the **N71** east to Connonagh, then turn northwest on an unclassified road to reach the **R586 (T65)**. Turn northeast for Dunmanway.*

## Dunmanway, Co Cork

**5** The famous Gaelic Athletic Association figure, Sam Maguire, was born near this early 17th-century linen industry plantation town and is buried in St Mary's cemetery.

There are fine forest walks at **Clashnacrona Woods**, 3 miles (5km) southwest of the town on the R586, and at **Aultagh Wood**, 4 miles (6km) north on the R587 (L58).

*Take the unclassified Coolkellure road northwest, then turn left on meeting the **R584 (L40)** and continue to Kealkill. Turn northeast on the **R584** through the Pass of Keimaneigh to reach the signposted Gougane Barra road.*

## Gougane Barra Forest Park, Co Cork

**6** The River Lee rises in Gougane Barra lake, a corrie lake surrounded by thickly wooded crags. Before moving on to the marshes of Cork, St Finbar had a hermitage in

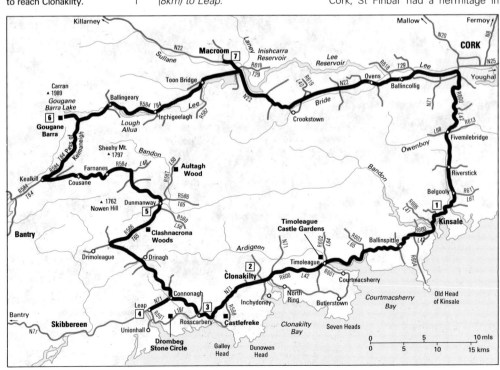

this remote spot. **St Finbar's Holy Island**, a small islet in the lake connected to the shore by a causeway, holds a tiny **Romanesque** chapel built in 1901. Pilgrimages are made to the hermitage each September.

Gougane Barra was Ireland's first forest park and is a haven of serenity.

*Drive northeast on the **R584** **(T64)** to Macroom, turning left on to the **N22** to enter the town.*

### Macroom, Co Cork

**7** Macroom Castle, just off the town square of this market town for the Gaelic-speaking region to the west, dates from the 13th century and was a seat of the MacCarthys of Muskerry. Oliver Cromwell granted it to Admiral Sir William Penn, whose son William spent much of his

*Just off Macroom town square is the castle, which dates from the 13th century. It was given to the father of William Penn, who spent much of his childhood here before emigrating to America*

childhood here and later founded the state of Pennsylvania in the United States. The admiral may have been born in the castle, but little now remains of it, although its impressive entrance has been restored.

*Take the **N22** east for 25 miles (40km) and return to Cork.*

Cork – Kinsale **16 (26)**
Kinsale – Clonakilty **22 (35)**
Clonakilty – Rosscarbery **8 (13)**
Rosscarbery – Leap **5 (8)**
Leap – Dunmanway **17 (27)**
Dunmanway – Gougane Barra **28 (45)**
Gougane Barra – Macroom **22 (35)**
Macroom – Cork **25 (40)**

### RECOMMENDED WALKS

*Cork, Co Cork* Cork has a Tourist Trail marked out for visitors and a copy can be obtained from the Tourist Information Office. (See also Tour 7.)

### FOR CHILDREN

*Cork, Co Cork* Treat the children to a cruise of Cork harbour. Departing from Kennedy Pier in nearby Cobh (see Tour 7), the cruiser passes harbour forts, Spike Island, the naval base, and ships of all descriptions from freighters to pleasure-boats.

**6** *Gougane Barra, Co Cork* Plan a picnic in Gougane Barra and let the children ramble through woodland paths and along the lakeside.

# UNSPOILED PENINSULAS

Bantry • Drimoleague • Skibbereen • Schull
Mizen Head • Durrus • Bantry

*The ferry to Shirkin Island leaving Baltimore harbour. On the island there are caves, sandy beaches, and the ruins of an abbey and castle*

### Drimoleague, Co Cork

**1** The Roman Catholic church in this small town is noteworthy for its architecture, a modern box-like structure with a solid, unbroken wall on one side, and glass on the other.

Castle Donovan, north of town and now in ruins, is a relic of the late 15th and early 16th centuries.

*Turn right on to the R593 (L59) and drive 8 miles (13km) south to Skibbereen.*

### Skibbereen, Co Cork

**2** This progressive town sits on the River Ilen just where it broadens and then empties into Baltimore Bay. Its long history of independence has produced two battling bishops – one who died fighting Elizabethan forces in 1602 and another who was hanged in 1650 during the Cromwellian conflicts.

The Maid of Erin monument in the town square was erected in 1904 by the Young Ireland Society. The Pro-Cathedral, a fine Grecian-style edifice built in 1826, is well worth a visit, while arts and crafts take centre stage at the West Cork Arts Centre.

Abbeystrewery Abbey, dating from the 14th century, lies in ruins 1 mile (1.5km) west of town, the setting for mass famine graves that bear silent witness to one of Ireland's most tragic eras.

Castletownshend, 5 miles (8km) southeast of Skibbereen via the R596 (L60), is a pretty little village with only one street that slopes rather steeply down to the sea. The tree that sits in the middle of that street was spared by roadmakers. This was home to Edith Somerville and Violet Martin Ross, two Victorian ladies whose humorous *Experiences of an Irish RM* has kept the entire English-speaking world chuckling. They lay buried in the Church of Ireland grounds, their

**B**antry sits at the head of one of Ireland's most beautiful bays, Bantry Bay. The bay has twice seen French attempts to invade it against the occupying English, in 1689 and 1796. The sheltered harbour that reaches right into the town centre is occupied by peaceful and picturesque fishing boats, and the narrow streets and broad square are lined with shops and houses that have changed little over the centuries.

*Bantry House*, a magnificent Georgian mansion dating back to 1739, is still home to descendants of Lord Bantry. The house, its landscaped grounds and impressive collections of art and antiques are open to the public. It is also the setting for the *French Armada Interpretive Centre*, which holds prints, documents, a cannon, and other artefacts from the ship that sank during the disastrous invasion of 1796.

*Kilnaruane Pillar Stone* in Rope Walk Road on the site of an early Celtic church (near the West Lodge Hotel), is a fine example of 7th-century carving and is thought to depict the ship of the church sailing upwards on its heavenly voyage.

*Take the N71 south and watch for the signposted turnoff to Drimoleague, 8 miles (13km) east via the R586 (T65).*

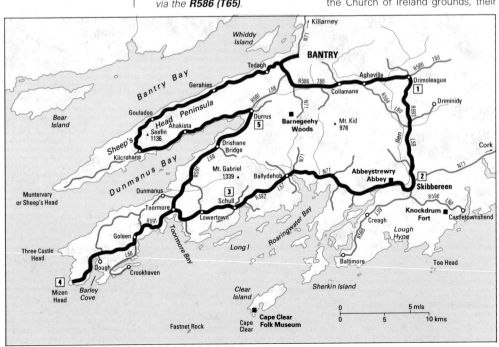

*Bantry House has a magnificent position by the sea. It is set in Italianate gardens and houses an extensive art collection*

lively spirits no doubt still haunting the halls of their beloved **Drishane House** at the upper end of the village. Just outside town, on a ridge overlooking the sea, **Knockdrum ring fort** has an underground passage (souterrain) and a stone with megalithic cup marks.

Eight miles (13km) southwest of Skibbereen, the little fishing village of **Baltimore** also has a stormy history, attested to by the ancient **castle** of the O'Driscolls, now in ruins, that still keeps a brooding eye on things from its perch on a rock overlooking the harbour. Despite the presence of that powerful clan, in 1631 Algerian pirates captured some 200 town residents for sale to North African slave traders and massacred most of those left behind. Poet Thomas Davis' *The Sack of Baltimore* gives a vivid account of the raid.

There are fine views of the bay and **Sherkin Island** from the tall white-washed navigational beacon a short distance outside the village, and there is a regular boat service from Baltimore to Sherkin Island, which defines the westward side of Baltimore Bay. **Silver Strand** is typical of several good swimming spots among the island's many coves. Of special note is the outstanding **Marine Research Centre** on this island.

Near the pier stand ruins of another **castle** of the O'Driscolls, destroyed in 1537, and on the eastern end of the island are remains of a **friary** founded by one of the O'Driscolls in the 15th century for the Franciscan Order of Strict Observance.

Southwest of Sherkin is **Clear Island**, one of the four Gaeltacht (Irish-speaking) areas in the Cork/Kerry region, with a regular boat service from Sherkin and mailboat service from Baltimore. This large island holds one of Europe's few electricity-generating windmills, an innovative EC pilot scheme. You will be well rewarded by a visit to the **Cape Clear Folk Museum.** There is also a small bird observatory that has tracked the migrations of a host of interesting species. Just south of the island, on the southernmost offshore point in Ireland, **Fastnet Rock Lighthouse** stands as a major navigational aid to mariners. This is the second light-house to occupy the rock, and was built in Cornwall in 1906 from local granite, disassembled and refitted on to the Fastnet Rock, each granite block dovetailed into the next in order to withstand the fierce seas surrounding the rock.

ℹ️ Town Hall

*Take the **N71** west to Ballydehob, then turn southwest on to the **R592 (L57)** to reach Schull, 14 miles (23km)*

### Schull, Co Cork

**3** The scenic drive west from Skibbereen follows the River Ilen and then the shore of **Roaringwater Bay** to Ballydehob, a picturesque little harbour that has attracted scores of craftspeople, whose workshops may well prompt a shopping stop. During World War II a German war plane crashed on the slopes of Mount Gabriel, which is now topped by an aircraft tracking station. Beautiful **Cuss Strand**, 2 miles (3km) from Ballydehob, offers excellent swimming. Further on, Schull's harbour is virtually enclosed, making it a haven for fishing and pleasure boats. This delightful little town usually has music in the pubs and a variety of resort-type special events during summer months. In the village, the **Church of Ireland church** (no longer in use) incorporates interesting medieval remains, and in the grounds of the Community College, a newly constructed, 60-seat **planetarium** is the

first of its kind in the Republic of Ireland. There is also a regular service to Clear Island from Schull.

*Follow the **R592 (L57)** to Toormore, then turn left on to the **R591 (L56)** to Goleen. At Goleen take an unclassified road to Mizen Head.*

### Mizen Head, Co Cork

**4** This part of the peninsula route calls out for a leisurely drive as it sweeps around beautiful Toormore Bay to **Goleen**, where a lovely secluded beach invites a break for a swim. From Goleen, you can either proceed straight out to Mizen Head via a minor road off the R591 (L56) or make a short side trip to the village of **Crookhaven**, whose charming harbour is a favourite with yachtsmen, before proceeding on to land's end. The fine sandy beaches of **Barley Cove** are a strong point in favour of the side trip to this popular resort spot. The drive on to Mizen Head is one of breathtaking seascapes and high vertical cliffs against which breaking white-foamed waves beat ceaselessly. Although the lighthouse at this southernmost mainland point

*Baltimore Bay looking towards Shirkin Island. This part of the coast is a popular sailing centre, and is also rich in wildlife*

*The coast near Goleen, Dunmanus Bay, where a gentle landscape slopes down to the sea*

of the country is not open to the public, the walk across the headland is exhilarating and provides a closer look at the spectacular cliffscapes that have lined the driving route. Exercise extreme caution, however, as the clifftops end abruptly and the fall is straight down.

*An unmarked road strikes north at Barley Cove, but is rough driving. The recommended route is a return to Goleen, where you rejoin the R591 (L56) north to Toormore, then turn northeast for the scenic drive to Durrus, 21 miles (34km).*

### Durrus, Co Cork

**5** Situated at the head of Dunmanus Bay, this village is the gateway to the narrow, 15-mile (24km) long **Sheep's Head Peninsula**. A minor, un-numbered road leads southwest

along the coast to the wooded inlet of **Ahakista**, where there is good swimming at sandy beaches and the **Air India Memorial** commemorating the loss of the passengers and crew when the plane crashed off this coast in 1985. Then on to **Kilcrohane**, which also has a good beach. Adventurous souls may want to continue south-west to the car-park from which you can walk to the Sheep's Head headland.

*At Kilcrohane, take the road known as Goat's Path across Seefin (Fionn's Seat) Mountain, the highest on the peninsula, for the drive along the southern shore of Bantry Bay. Just past the village of Tedagh, turn left on to the N71 for the short drive back to Bantry.*

Bantry – Drimoleague 11 (18)
Drimoleague – Skibbereen 8 (13)
Skibbereen – Schull 14 (23)
Schull – Mizen Head 18 (29)
Mizen Head – Durrus 21 (34)
Durrus – Bantry 24 (39)

### SPECIAL TO ...

This West Cork region is alive with festivals and special events during summer months. There are regattas in Castletownshend and Schull in July and Baltimore, Schull and Crookhaven in August. In July and August, Castletownshend holds its **Festival of Music**; Skibbereen celebrates its **Maid of the Isles Festival**; and Schull has a festival just on principle. Skibbereen also has its **Harness and Trotting Grand Prix** in August. The entire area is also a mecca for anglers, with sea and shore angling, and salmon fishing in the River Ilen at Skibbereen. Trout are the prize at lakes Garranes and Driminidy near Drimoleague.

**2 days – 147 miles (235km)**

# ROCK OF CASHEL

Waterford ● Passage East ● Dunmore East ● Tramore
Dungarvan ● Cappoquin ● Lismore ● Cahir ● Cashel
Clonmel ● Carrick-on-Suir ● Waterford

Waterford is the most important seaport of the southeast and also reflects much of the country's history. *Reginald's Tower*, reputedly built by Reginald McIvor in 1003, stands sentinel on The Quay, where today its *museum* guards Waterford's historical treasures. Traces of the old Viking-built city walls can be seen at the railway station, Mayor's Walk and Castle Street. *Christ Church Cathedral*, established in 1050 by the same Reginald McIvor, is at the top of Henrietta Street, although the present building dates from the 18th century. On Greyfriars Street, the ruins of the *French Church* are all that remains of a 13th-century Franciscan Foundation which later became a hospital. The *Waterford Heritage Centre* in Greyfriars Street features archaeology in Waterford, with particular emphasis on the period AD1000–1500, including a model of medieval Waterford. The *Waterford Crystal Glass Factory*, on the *N25* (Cork road), is a modern industrial complex that creates fine works in glass. The lovely old Victorian *Theatre Royal* on The Mall is the venue for theatricals, and during the summer months there are river cruises and guided walking tours.

*Lismore Castle has a commanding position overlooking the Blackwater river. It was built in 1185 by King John and is one of several reminders of the city's medieval past*

ⓘ 41 The Quay

*From Waterford take the **R683 (L157)** east for 8 miles (13km) to Passage East.*

### Passage East, Co Waterford

**1** This quaint riverside village with its whitewashed cottages, narrow, winding streets and a car-ferry service to Ballyhack, County Wexford, was the landing point for Henry II, who arrived in 1171 with 4,000 men in 400 ships to receive oaths of loyalty from Irish chieftains who wished to hold on to their lands. The hill just above the village provides splendid views of the head of Waterford harbour.

On the road to Dunmore East are the ruins of **Geneva Barracks**, relics of a colony of goldsmiths and silversmiths from Switzerland who sought refuge from religious persecution and settled here in 1782. Their planned town of New Geneva was a failure, and by 1785 the site was abandoned. The barracks were used as a prison for insurgents (or 'croppies') of the 1798 rising, subjects of the ballad 'The Croppy Boy'.

*Follow an unclassified coastal road south and on joining the **R684 (L158)** turn left for 3 miles (5km) for Dunmore East.*

### Dunmore East, Co Waterford

**2** Neat thatched cottages perch on steep hills above the harbour in this pretty little village that is a popular summer resort and sea angling centre. Pleasure boats and fishing vessels fill the picturesque harbour. The bay is divided by projecting headlands broken into cliffs and

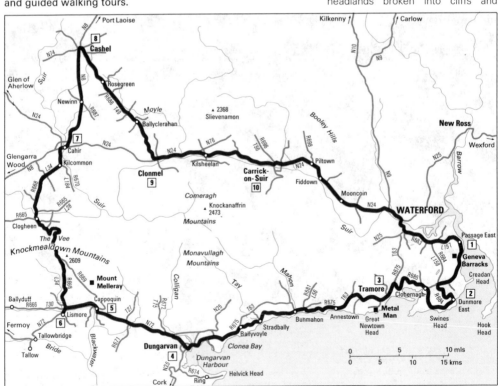

The coastline between Tramore and Dungarvan is characterised by rocky headlands and coves

coves, with good walks to **Creadan Head** to the north, **Black Knob** promontory to the south, and **Swines Head** at the southern end of the peninsula. There are also several safe sandy beaches in the area.

*Take an unclassified coastal road to the junction with the **R685**, turn left, then left again at the junction with the **R675 (T63)** and continue for 2 miles (3km) to Tramore.*

### Tramore, Co Waterford

**3** This lively seaside town is one of the southeast coast's most popular resorts with a wide, 3-mile-long (5km) beach, its water warmed by the Gulf Stream. Attractions include a 50-acre (20-hectare) **amusement park**, a **race course**, miniature golf, and an 18-hole golf course. Surfing is a popular watersport here, and there is good swimming at the pier, **Guillameen Cove** and **Newton Cove**.

The giant clifftop 'Metal Man' statue at Great Newtown Head, south of town, was erected as a navigational landmark for sailors, and legend has it that any unmarried female who hops around it three times will hop down the aisle within 12 months.

On the coastal drive to Dungarvan, the little fishing village of **Bunmahon** has a good sandy beach surrounded by jagged cliffs that rise to about 200 feet (60m), with interesting rock formations at their base.

*From Tramore, follow the **R675** coastal drive via Stradbally for 25 miles (40km) southwest to Dungarvan.*

### Dungarvan, Co Waterford

**4** A busy market town, Dungarvan sits on the broad, natural harbour where the Colligan river meets the sea. Along the quays can be seen remnants of **Dungarvan Castle**, dating from 1186, surrounded by fortified walls. At the top of Main Street an excellent small **museum**, with prints, documents and artefacts of Dungarvan's turbulent history through colonial and revolutionary eras, is located in the **Old Market House**, which dates from 1642. Five miles (8km) south of town on the R674 is the village of **Ring**, where Irish is the daily language and is taught in an acclaimed language college. Further east beyond Ring, impressive **Helvick Head** rises to 230 feet (70m) and shelters a picturesque small harbour.

*Take the **R672 (T75)**, then the **N72** west to Cappoquin.*

### Cappoquin, Co Waterford

**5** The broad Blackwater river makes a 90-degree turn to the west at Cappoquin, and provides scenic riverside drives and some of the best salmon fishing, trout angling and coarse fishing in Ireland.

Four miles (6km) north of Cappoquin, via the R669, in the foothills of the Knockmealdown Mountains, **Mount Melleray** is a monastic centre for the Cistercian Order of the Strict Observance, built well over a century ago by monks who had been banished from France. The Order erected an impressive stone church and outbuildings and has transformed a bare mountainside into productive fields and pastures.

*Follow the **N72** for 4 miles (6km) to Lismore.*

## FOR HISTORY BUFFS

**8** *Cashel, Co Tipperary*
In the 5th century, a cashel, or stone fort, was erected on the lofty Rock of Cashel, and it was here, legend has it, that St Patrick came to preach to the King of Munster, using the humble shamrock as a symbol of the Christian trinity. In 1101, Murtough O'Brien presented the Cashel of the Kings to the Church. In 1127, Cormac MacCarthaigh, King of Desmond, built the little chapel, a miniature gem of Romanesque style. King Henry II came here to receive homage from Irish princes; Edward the Bruce held a parliament here; and the first Protestant service was conducted here.

## FOR CHILDREN

**3** *Tramore, Co Waterford*
Children will love the **amusement park** at Tramore, as well as the miniature railway, and the broad, curving beach.

**4** *Dungarvan, Co Waterford*
Further south on the coastal drive, **Clonea Strand**, some 2 miles (3km) east of Dungarvan, flies the European blue flag for cleanliness, and there are ample refreshment facilities.

## SCENIC ROUTES

There is scarcely a mile of this tour that could not be described as a scenic route. The **R675**, the coastal road from Tramore to Dungarvan, dips and winds through the quaint little fishing villages of **Annestown** and **Bunmahon**, with spectacular seascapes of soaring cliffs and quiet little coves. A short detour to the wide, curving beach at **Clonea Strand** is worthwhile. The Vee drive from Lismore to Clogheen, on the **R668**, winds and twists along mountainsides covered with heather to the V-shaped pass in the Knockmealdown Mountains, with lay-bys giving sweeping views of Tipperary's Golden Vale, before descending to the little town of Clogheen. Between the pass and Clogheen, look for the stone cairn on the northern slope, where Samuel Grubb of Grace Castle was interred upright overlooking his landholdings. This drive is especially spectacular in the spring when the mountainsides are ablaze with rhododendron flowers.

## BACK TO NATURE

**7** *Cahir, Co Tipperary* The 1 mile (1.5km) nature trail in **Glengarra Wood** is a delight for nature lovers interested in rare and exotic trees and plants. To reach the wood, drive 8 miles (13km) southwest of Cahir via the **N8**, and turn right on to the signposted and unclassified road, then continue 2 miles (3km) to the car-park. There are nature walks along the Burncourt river and through forest groves, where Douglas fir, several types of fern and native heathers, Western hemlock, rowan, holly, birch, arboreal rhododendron, Bhutan pine from the Inner Himalayas of eastern India, and many other unusual plants and trees can be seen. Native birds such as the treecreeper, the tiny goldcrest, wren, robin, chaffinch, magpie, jay and the introduced pheasant make this their home, as do fallow deer.

## Lismore, Co Waterford

**6** Set on the Blackwater river, Lismore's most prominent feature is **Lismore Castle**, which looms over town and river, looking for all the world like something out of a fairytale. It was built by King John in 1185 on the site of a 7th-century monastery that became one of Europe's most renowned seats of learning. After surviving devastating attacks by Viking raiders, the monastic university finally succumbed to the assaults of Raymond le Gros in 1173. The castle was presented to Sir Walter Raleigh, who sold it to Richard Boyle, Earl of Cork, in 1602. His son, Robert, the noted chemist and author of Boyle's Law, was born here. Since 1753 it has been the Irish seat of the Dukes of Devonshire, and the gardens are open to the public. The medieval **Protestant cathedral** dates from 1633, although it was largely rebuilt around 1680. It has soaring Gothic vaulting and still retains its west wall 9th- and 11th-century grave slabs from an earlier church. The modern (1888) **Catholic cathedral** is Romanesque in style.

Five miles (8km) south of Lismore, via the N72, the little town of **Tallow**

*The road from Lismore to Cahir climbs and twists through the Knockmealdown Mountains, through a pass called The Vee, which provides stunning and extensive views of the Golden Vale of Tipperary. The stone cairn marks the burial spot of Samuel Grubb*

was the birthplace of famed 19th-century sculptor John Hogan. Splendid panoramic views open up from 592-foot (180m) **Tallow Hill**, less than 1 mile (1.5km) northeast of town, and there are ruins of an ancient fortified **Fitzgerald keep** ½ mile (1km) west of Tallowbridge.

Six miles (10km) west of Lismore, via the **R666 (T30)**, the quaint village of **Ballyduff** is a popular angling centre and also holds the ruins of **Mocollop Castle**, another Fitzgerald fortress.

*At the eastern end of the bridge in Lismore take the **R668 (L34)** which follows the Blackwater river, then climbs to the pass in the Knockmealdown Mountains known as The Vee and descends to Clogheen, continuing on to Cahir.*

*The Rock of Cashel is a limestone mound 200 feet (60m) high. It is topped by the ruins of Cormac's Tower, St Patrick's Cathedral and the Round Tower, which is 92 feet (30m) high*

### Cahir, Co Tipperary

**7** Cahir Castle, with its massive great hall, grim dungeon, and thick protective enclosing walls, is a superb restoration of the 1142 castle set on a rocky islet in the River Suir. It is also one of Ireland's best preserved castles. Furnishings in the residential apartments are authentic reproductions of the period. The Articles ending the long Cromwellian wars were signed here in 1652, and in modern times it has served as a setting for such films as *Excalibur* and *Barry Lyndon*. Cahir is a centre for walking and climbing.

A few miles (km) northwest of Cahir, the N8 (the road to Tipperary town) leads to the left turnoff heading to the lush **Glen of Aherlow**, a secluded place that was once a major route between the counties of Tipperary and Limerick and the scene of ancient battles. Later, Irish insurgents and outlaws took refuge in this thickly wooded valley running between the Galtee Mountains and Slievenamuck Hills.

*From Cahir, follow the **N8** due north for 12 miles (19km) to Cashel.*

### Cashel, Co Tipperary

**8** Dominating the landscape for miles around is the awe-inspiring **Rock of Cashel** which soars 200 feet (60m) above the surrounding plains. Since ancient Celtic times, its 2-acre (0.8-hectare) summit has been connected with royalty and mysticism. **Cormac's Chapel**, the **Round Tower**, **St Patrick's Cathedral**, and a replica of **St Patrick's Cross** (whose base may actually have been a pre-Christian sacrificial altar), are among the impressive ruins, all in remarkably good condition. At the foot of the Rock, a visitors' centre of stylised Celtic design presents traditional Irish entertainment.

*Take the **R688 (T49)** southeast for 15 miles (24km) to Clonmel.*

### Clonmel, Co Tipperary

**9** Set on the banks of the River Suir, Clonmel is the main town of County Tipperary, where the world's first public transport system was established by Charles Bianconi in 1815, based at Hearn's Hotel in Parnell Street. Parts of the 19th-century **Franciscan church** in Abbey Street go back to the 13th century. The 19th-century **St Mary's Church** nearby is notable for its fine high altar. The gallery in the **Library** has good coin and military displays and paintings by 20th-century Irish artists.

Note also the well-preserved old **West Town Wall**, on Mary Street. The town's streets are lined with restored shopfronts.

*Take the **N24** east for 14 miles (23km) to Carrick-on-Suir.*

### Carrick-on-Suir, Co Tipperary

**10** This scenic little town is set on the River Suir, and its **Ormonde Castle** is the only Elizabethan fortified mansion of its kind in Ireland. One of the principal seats of the Butlers, the earls and dukes of Ormonde, it is said to have been built by the legendary 'Black Tom', Earl of Ormonde, to host Elizabeth I, who proceeded to cancel her visit.

Despite their power and influence with the Crown, however, the Ormonde's were not able to prevent the arrest of the Archbishop of Cashel, who was taken prisoner here and martyred in Dublin in 1584.

*Take the **N24** for the 17 miles (27km) back to Waterford.*

| | |
|---|---|
| Waterford – Passage East | **8 (13)** |
| Passage East – Dunmore East | **9 (14)** |
| Dunmore East – Tramore | **11 (18)** |
| Tramore – Dungarvan | **25 (40)** |
| Dungarvan – Cappoquin | **10 (16)** |
| Cappoquin – Lismore | **4 (6)** |
| Lismore – Cahir | **22 (35)** |
| Cahir – Cashel | **12 (19)** |
| Cashel – Clonmel | **15 (24)** |
| Clonmel – Carrick-on-Suir | **14 (23)** |
| Carrick-on-Suir – Waterford | **17 (27)** |

---

**RECOMMENDED WALKS**

**3** *Tramore, Co Waterford*
At Tramore, the pleasant oceanfront promenade leads to a range of sandhills known as **The Burrows**. West of town, both the **Garrarus Strand** and the **Kilfarrasy Strand** are pleasant seaside walks. To the southwest of town, there are walks along the Doneraile cliffs.

**9** *Clonmel, Co Tipperary*
From Clonmel, you can walk the 12-mile (19km) towpath to Carrick-on-Suir.

---

**SPECIAL TO ...**

*Waterford, Co Waterford*
In September, a lighthearted gathering of amateur companies from around the world and from all parts of Ireland converge on Waterford for the annual **International Festival of Light Opera**. For 16 nights there are performances of such musicals as *Brigadoon* and *Showboat*, all to a very high standard.

# LEINSTER

Leinster might well be called the 'Royal Province' of Ireland. Its 12 counties have harboured rulers from the days of the prehistoric clans who constructed the great burial mound at Newgrange to the High Kings of Ireland who ruled from the Hill of Tara, from Viking and Norman conquerors, to appointees of English kings and queens. Indeed, with Irish chieftains battling against invaders and each other around the country, it seemed best to concentrate beleaguered Crown forces in 'The Pale' a heavily fortified area around Dublin.

At Clontarf, just outside Dublin, the great Irish High King, Brian Boru defeated the Vikings in 1014. In 1649, Oliver Cromwell arrived with his dreaded 'ironside' forces and proceeded to march from Dublin to Drogheda, where he slaughtered thousands of men, women and children. And in 1690, William of Orange's decisive victory at the Battle of the Boyne had a profound effect on Ireland's history that echoes down the centuries to the present day.

South of 'The Pale', County Wexford bears the scars of Viking occupation followed by Normans, whose first landing in Ireland was along this county's coast. Cromwell and the insurgents of 1798 left their imprint on this lovely county. The lush countryside of Kilkenny lured Normans by the score, who dotted the landscape with their castles and built a dignified town that soon rivalled Dublin as an administrative centre.

Inland, Athlone stands guard over County West-meath's rural, lake-dotted landscape and the River Shannon that divides it from Connacht. Along the banks of that great waterway in County Offaly are the remains of one of Ireland's most awe-inspiring ecclesiastical settlements, Clonmacnoise. Kildare's Hill of Allen is thought to have been the winter quarters of Fionn MacCumhail's (Finn MacCool's) legendary Fianna warriors, but these days the county is known for its famous stud farms and Curragh race course.

The lushness and variety of Leinster's landscape are as much a delight to today's visitors as they were to past conquerors, many of whom sprinkled it with great mansions and gardens. The lake-filled midland counties draw avid fisherpeople and boaters on the Shannon, and the seemingly inexhaustible bogs of counties Laois and Offaly yield peat to fuel 40 per cent of the Republic's electricity. Along the coast are curving bays and sandy beaches, as well as nature reserves inhabited by a wide range of birds and wildlife.

## Tour 11

From the historically important Athlone and its modern-day river-boating, this tour takes you to the former garrison town of Mullingar, whose proximity to good trout lakes makes it an excellent angling centre. Then you travel to Tullamore, home of a world-famous distillery, and on to Birr, with its castle and garden. The monastic ruins of Clonmacnoise lend a spiritual aspect to your travels, as do the ruins at Ballinasloe.

## Tour 12

This is an historic drive through Ireland's past, in pleasant country-side rich in megalithic and early Christian monuments, including the intriguing masterpieces of the pas-sage grave of Newgrange, exquisite high crosses at Monasterboice, Slane and its associations with St Patrick and the Hill of Tara, redolent of the heroic age of the high kings of Ireland. The tour ends with the site of the Battle of the Boyne in 1690, where King William met King James to finish a conflict of national and European significance.

## Tour 13

From the Georgian elegance of Dublin, the tour visits bright coastal towns which owe much of their character to Victorian enthusiasm for the seaside. The route winds its way into the mountains, and visits Glendalough, one of Ireland's most captivating combinations of history and landscape. The scenery, which follows combines bog, lake and mountain top, and a highlight of this

*Above: Looking towards Dalkey Island, south of Dublin*
*Right: The ruins of a monastic settlement at Monasterboice, dating back to the 5th century*

tour is the profusion of glorious gardens, justifying the claim that this area is 'the garden of Ireland'.

## Tour 14

Norman castles, ecclesiastical ruins and tales of medieval witches haunt Kilkenny, starting point for this tour. History and active river commerce meld happily in New Ross on the River Barrow. Further along the river, prehistory has left its mark just outside Carlow town in the form of an impressive dolmen. Kildare's horse country will appeal to followers of the sport of kings, and beautiful gardens near Port Laoise have universal appeal. Celtic kings and St Patrick draw you on to Cashel.

## Tour 15

Founded by Vikings, invaded by Normans, conquered by Cromwells troops, and a hotbed of insurgence, Wexford is an excellent tour base: north to the country's famed beaches, then inland for more history, before turning south to the river town of New Ross. South to Waterford, another Viking stronghold and the east coast's most important port, then a ferry ride to the enchanting Hook Peninsula takes you through villages virtually undisturbed by 'progress', and on to a noted bird refuge and a holy island.

**1/2 days – 141 miles (227km)**

# MONASTIC RUINS & THE MIDLANDS

Athlone ● Mullingar ● Tullamore ● Birr ● Clonmacnoise
Ballinasloe ● Athlone

Athlone is important as a major marketing and transportation centre, a junction for highway, rail, and river traffic. Its *marina* is a mecca for those longing to cruise the Shannon, with fleets of smart river cruisers for hire with or without experienced boatmen (beginners are given instruction before setting sail). Fisherpeople and golfers also gravitate to Athlone, which has good facilities for both.

*Adamson Castle,* overlooking the bridge, is a 13th-century structure, and there are marvellous town views from loopholes in the 40-foot-high (12m) curtain wall. The interesting *museum* inside contains relics of the town and district's history, and there is an informative Visitor Centre. The *Church of Saints Peter and Paul* is an impressive building with soaring twin spires that dominate the town's skyline and a graceful dome. *St Anthony's Friary,* by contrast, is of Irish-Romanesque architecture and features an unusual round tower belfry.

*Athlone Crystal,* which has taken a leading place in Ireland's burgeoning crystal industry, has workshops and showrooms of interest to shoppers.

*Locke's Distillery at Kilbeggan. Built in the 18th century, it has recently been restored and houses a museum, antiques shop and café*

*Take the **N55** northeast for 26 miles (42km) to the town of Edgeworthstown, then turn southeast on to the **N4** for the 18-mile (29km) drive to Mullingar.*

## Mullingar, Co Westmeath

**1** En route to Mullingar, stop by the small **museum** dedicated to the Edgeworths family in **Edgeworthstown**. The father of the family was a noted inventor and author, and his daughter Maria, although English-born, became one of Ireland's leading women writers. She holds a special place in Irish affections for her work among the suffering during the famine years. Edgeworthstown also has an excellent small **historical museum**.

If you plan to eat steak in Ireland, Mullingar is the place to do it, in the very heart of Ireland's cattle raising area. The county town of Westmeath, Mullingar's long history includes a position of prime importance as a barracks town for the British military. During the Williamite Wars, it was here that British commander de Ginkel rallied his forces for the 1691 siege of Athlone. The imprint of those years is stamped on the town's face even today in the form of large, grey, rather formidable buildings. The present-day personality of the town, however, in no way reflects its somewhat grim past, and Mullingar is an excellent base for seeing the County Westmeath lakes, most of which offer excellent brown trout fishing.

*Impressive Birr Castle occupies a commanding position. The central tower of an earlier castle on the site has been incorporated into the house*

The **Cathedral of Christ the King**, designed by Ralph Byrne, has outstanding mosaics of St Patrick and St Anne near the high altar that are the work of Russian artist, Boris Anrep. Permission must be obtained from the sacristan to see the ecclesiastical museum above the sacristy.

Interesting memorabilia of Mullingar's barracks years, as well as Irish Army participation in UN activities in the Lebanon, Cyprus, and the Congo, are displayed in the **Columb Barracks' Military and Historical Museum**.

Cloudy ancient mirrors, original order books, and a little-changed interior are all reminders that **Canten Casey's Pub** is 200 years old – a unique look back into Ireland's past.

Travel in almost any direction from Mullingar and you can find the lakes that have made this region famous for trout. **Lough Ennell** is about 6 miles (10km) to the south, with a championship golf course overlooking the lake and the ruins of ancient **Lynn Church** on its northeastern shore. Three miles (5km) north of town, **Lough Owel** is a sailing and sub aqua centre, and there are good swimming facilities. About 6 miles (10km) north of town, **Lough Derravaragh** is a beautiful, irregular-shaped lake with thickly wooded shores. It plays a central part in one of Ireland's most tragic and beloved legends, since it was one of three lakes on which the Children of Lir were doomed to spend 300 years when their wicked stepmother turned them into swans. Swans on Irish waters are still under the protection granted all swans by the grieving father.

For good views of the lakes and surrounding plains, **Rathconnell Hill** is just 2 miles (3km) northeast of Mullingar off the N52. Lough Owel is part of the view from 499-foot (152m) Shanemore (Slanemore) Hill, 4 miles (6km) northwest of town.

Thirteen miles (21km) north of Mullingar via the R394, **Tullynally Castle and Gardens**, in Castlepollard, are one of County Westmeath's chief attractions. Seat of the Earls of Longford since the 17th century, the turreted and towered Gothic-revival manor house has a two-storey Great Hall with a vaulted ceiling and impressive collections of art, china and furnishings. Life 'downstairs' in such a great house is depicted in the **museum** housed in the courtyard, Victorian kitchens and laundries. The 30-acre (12-hectare) grounds offer woodland walks, a water garden and Victorian grotto.

The village of **Fore**, about 3 miles (5km) east of **Castlepollard**, is the setting for an interesting group of antiquities. Before exploring, stop at the **Abbey Pub** to see paintings of the 'Seven Wonders of Fore'. Partly restored **St Fechin's Church** is a fine example of early church architecture, with a massive lintel stone on the west door that legend says was placed there by the saint himself. Then there is the **Benedictine priory** whose loophole windows and square towers give it the look of a castle; the 'Holy Trinity tree' that has never had but three branches; the **spring** beside the tree whose water never boils; and **St Fechin's Mill**, with a miraculous underground water supply. To the east of the village, there is a large motte thought to be an early Anglo-Norman fortification, and within a one-mile (1.5km) radius there are nine ancient crosses.

*i* Dublin Road (**N4**)

*Continue south for 22 miles (35km) on the **N52** for Tullamore.*

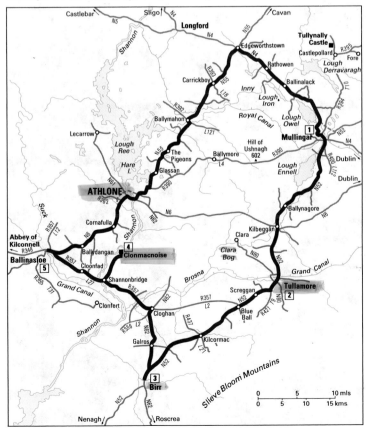

## BACK TO NATURE

**2** *Tullamore, Co Offaly* About 7 miles (11km) northwest of Tullamore, **Clara Bog** is one of the largest intact raised bogs of its type in Ireland. Its well developed 'soak' system is considered to be the best in western Europe. Increased water flow from surface run-off or underground springs allows the growth of many more plant species than are normally found in a bog environment. Among those that thrive here are bog mosses, sundews, heathers, cotton grass, and bog rosemary. There are hummock/hollow complexes, bog pools and moss lawns. The bog is easily seen from the road, but is considered unsafe to explore on foot.

## RECOMMENDED WALKS

*Athlone, Co Westmeath* On Lough Ree's western shore, about 8 miles (13km) from Athlone, **Rinndown Peninsula** juts out into the lake just east of the village of **Lecarrow**. Follow the unnumbered road from Lecarrow until it becomes a track leading to the lakeshore. The heavily wooded path passes ancient ruins from the 13th century that combine with the dense shade to create a somewhat spooky atmosphere. The walk takes in the remains of **St John's Castle** (so named for the Knights of St John who once occupied it) and a church with its outbuildings.

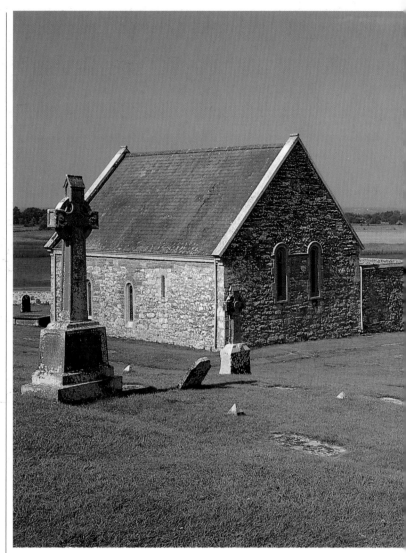

### Tullamore, Co Offaly

**2** On the drive from Mullingar, stop off at the village of Kilbeggan, 7 miles (11km) north of Tullamore, where a museum, antiques shop, and café now occupy the restored 18th-century Locke's Distillery, once one of Europe's largest.

The chief town of County Offaly, Tullamore owes its development to the Grand Canal laid out in 1798 to connect Dublin to the Shannon. The canal carried huge cargoes of yellow brick made in the town to Dublin during its expansion in the 19th century.

Tullamore has gained international fame as home of the Irish Mist Distillery, producers of Ireland's leading liqueur whiskey. The distillery presents a video and tasting on weekdays.

St Catherine's is the fine Gothic-style church you see perched on top of Hop Hill overlooking the town.

*Follow the N52 for 23 miles (37km) southwest to Birr.*

### Birr, Co Offaly

**3** Plan a stop in the village of Kilcormac, about 12 miles (19km) southwest of Tullamore on the N52, for a look at the beautifully carved wooden pietà in the Catholic church, which is thought to be the work of a 16th century artist.

Attractive Georgian buildings and a world famous castle and garden are the main attractions in the small town of Birr, just above the confluence of the Little Brosna and Camcor rivers.

Birr Castle is an impressive fortified manor house set in extensive grounds. Only the grounds are open to the public, since it has for several centuries been the residence of the earls of Rosse. The 3rd Earl was a noted astronomer, whose giant 72-inch (180cm) reflecting telescope, built to his own design in 1845, was the largest in the world for an astounding 80 years. The walls and tube of that instrument are on view in a scientific museum in the grounds, along with other astronomical arte-facts, drawings, photographs, and a scale model of the original telescope. The castle gardens cover 100 acres (40 hectares), laid out on the banks of the two rivers and around a lake. More than 1,000 species of plants and trees include magnolias, cherry trees, chestnut trees and weeping beeches, as well as box hedges named as the tallest in the world by the Guinness Book of Records.

*Take the N62 north to Cloghan, and turn west on to the R357 to Shannonbridge. Then follow a signposted unclassified road north for 4 miles (6km) to Clonmacnoise.*

*Clonmacnoise is one of Ireland's most important religious sites. Remains of the 6th-century monastic settlement include a cathedral, eight churches, and over 200 monumental slabs*

## Clonmacnoise, Co Offaly

**4** Set beside the Shannon river, this is one of Ireland's holiest places. St Ciaran's monastery, founded here in 548, became the most famous of Ireland's monastic cities and was one of Europe's leading centres of learning for nearly 1,000 years. It enjoyed the patronage of many Irish Kings, and Rory O'Conor, the last High King, lies buried here. Its great fame and wealth attracted plunderers from home and abroad, and the final indignity came in 1552 when the English garrison at Athlone carried off spoils that included even the glass from the windows, and the site was finally abandoned. Restoration began in 1647, but Cromwellian forces carried out yet another raid that put paid to the revival of its former glory. Today, the site holds a **cathedral**, one of eight church ruins, two round towers, three sculptured high crosses (and parts of two others), over 200 monumental slabs and a ruined castle. St Ciaran's grave is said to be in the east end of 'The Little Church', a small 9th-century cell.

*Return to Shannonbridge and turn northwest on to the R357 (L27) for the 8-mile (13km) drive to Ballinasloe.*

## Ballinasloe, Co Galway

**5** Its strategic position and military importance in the past are attested to by the **castle** in Ballinasloe, although today it is a thriving market town. Seven miles (11km) from town on the Athenry road is the **Abbey of Kilconnell**, founded in 1400. Its nave, choir, side aisles, south transept, and some of the cloisters are in perfect condition.

Clonfert, 13 miles (21km) southeast of Ballinasloe, was the site chosen by St Brendan the Navigator in the 6th century for a monastic settlement. Nothing remains today, but the present church features outstanding Romanesque decoration, most notably the doorway, with a great variety of motifs, including animal and human heads and intricate carvings of foliage.

*Take the N6 northeast for 16 miles (26km) to return to Athlone.*

Athlone – Mullingar **44 (71)**
Mullingar – Tullamore **22 (35)**
Tullamore – Birr **23 (37)**
Birr – Clonmacnoise **22 (35)**
Clonmacnoise – Ballinasloe **14 (23)**
Ballinasloe – Athlone **16 (26)**

### SPECIAL TO ...

**4** *Clonmacnoise, Co Offaly*
Each year on 9 September and the following Sunday, great throngs, drawn from around the world, make the pilgrimage to Clonmacnoise to commemorate **St Ciaran's feast day.**

**5** *Ballinasloe, Co Galway*
Ballinasloe's great **October Fair** carries on for eight days of fierce trading, street entertainment, and non-stop revelry. It is one of the few such fairs still held in modern Ireland.

**2 days – 84 miles (134km)**

# THE BOYNE VALLEY

Drogheda ● Monasterboice ● Mellifont
Newgrange, Knowth and Dowth ● Slane ● Kells ● Navan
Tara ● Battle of the Boyne Site ● Drogheda

The great grassy mound of *Millmount*, which gives a panoramic view over Drogheda, was first a passage grave, then a Viking meeting place, a Norman motte, and an important military barracks in the 18th century, its history mirroring that of the town. Today, some of Millmount's buildings have been converted into a small *museum*.

A view from any point of the town will show you that Drogheda is a town of churches. *St Peter's* in West Street contains the head of Oliver Plunkett, martyred in 1681 at Tyburn and proclaimed a saint in 1975. *St Laurence's Gate* is an impressive barbican defence set up by the Norman Hugh de Lacy, part of a system of gates and walls that actually divided the town in two. The great railway viaduct across the Boyne, built in the middle of the 19th century, dominates the busy port.

*One of the impressive Celtic crosses in the village of Kells, home of the Book of Kells. Its carved scriptural message is still remarkably clear*

[i] Drogheda

*Take the **N1** for Belfast. After 5 miles (8km) turn left, following signposts for Boyne Drive, Monasterboice. In half a mile (1km) turn left again.*

**Monasterboice, Co Louth**

**1** Pick your way between ancient and modern graves to see two of the finest high crosses. These free standing carvings in stone are of a quality unparalleled anywhere in Europe at the time they were erected, and yet the very high round tower is a reminder that these remarkable works of art were executed in the midst of Viking plunder. The West Cross stands close to the round tower and the Cross of Muiredach, so called because of the inscription on the base, which says 'A prayer for Muiredach by whom this cross was made', is smaller and more perfect in appearance. The messages on these crosses follow coherent themes of God's grace to man and the parallels between Old and New Testaments. On Muiredach's cross look for the stories of Adam and Eve and Cain and Abel, the Last Judgement and the Crucifixion of Christ.

An event of religious significance of more recent times was the visit of Pope John Paul in 1979, and the point where he celebrated mass is marked on the main Belfast–Dublin road.

*The remains of Mellifont Abbey, the first Cistercian settlement to be founded in Ireland. Only fragments now remain, including an octagonal lavabo*

*Continue on past Monasterboice. After a mile (2km) turn right for Mellifont. After a mile (2km) turn left on to the Drogheda road, R168 (T25), and after a further mile (2km) turn right for Mellifont.*

## Mellifont, Co Louth

**2** In a pleasant valley beside the River Mattock, Malachy, the former Archbishop of Armagh, founded the first Cistercian monastery in Ireland in 1142. He had been inspired to emulate the church structures and architecture of his close friend, Bernard of Clairvaux. A substantial square gatehouse still stands, but only fragments of this greatest of Cistercian monasteries now remain, including arches of a Romanesque cloister and a chapter house. An octagonal lavabo once equipped with water jets and basins is the most interesting structure.

*Return to the crossroads and turn right. After 2 miles (3km) turn right. Go straight over the crossroads, following the signpost to King William's Glen. After a mile (1.5km) turn right on to the N51, then 2½ miles (4km) further on, turn left and follow signs for Newgrange.*

## Newgrange, Knowth and Dowth, Co Meath

**3** Irish architecture may be said to begin in the Boyne Valley, when, in about 3000BC, people who had only stone and wood for tools, created the most impressive monuments of their kind in western Europe. Little is known of these people, or of those interred in these prehistoric tombs, but excavations have shown that they were cultivators of crops and had cleared areas of forest.

The mound at Newgrange, constructed with water-rolled pebbles, rises to a height of 36 feet (11m), its mass retained by a kerb of great stone blocks lying end to end, topped by white quartz and granite boulders. The passage is lined by huge stones, and the central cross-shaped chamber is roofed with a vault untouched in five

millennnia. Standing around the mound is an incomplete circle of stones.

At Dowth a larger passage-tomb has two chambers, while Knowth has two passage-tombs surrounded by 18 smaller ones. Knowth was used from the Stone Age, and in the early Christian era was a seat of the High Kings of Ireland. The significance of the Boyne Valley tombs is that here art combines with the engineering feats of the passage-tombs of Ireland. Spirals, lozenges, zigzags, sunbursts – figures cut in stone with stone implements – decorate the monuments.

At Newgrange the sophisticated structure incorporates the unique phenomenon of a roof-box, which, only at the winter solstice, allows the rays of the rising sun to penetrate the chamber and flood it with light. Newgrange is shown by guided tours, and at busy times you will have to arrive early in the day to ensure admission. Archaeological work continues, and important discoveries are still being made in the Boyne Valley; at times sites may be closed for excavation.

*i* Newgrange

*Return by minor roads to the N51 and turn left for Slane, 6 miles (10km).*

## Slane, Co Meath

**4** Slane occupies an attractive curve on the River Boyne, and is overlooked by the Hill of Slane, where, tradition has it, St Patrick lit his paschal fire in AD433 in defiance of the orders of King Laoghaire. In his persuasive speech to the king, Patrick used the shamrock as his illustration of the Trinity. He won his argument and permission to preach Christianity throughout the land. From the view point on the hill, the pleasant village can be seen running steeply down to the river.

The mill by the banks of the Boyne houses a transport museum, and just to the east is the cottage of Francis Ledwidge, the poet who was killed during World War I.

Slane Castle has a magnificent Gothic ballroom specially built for the

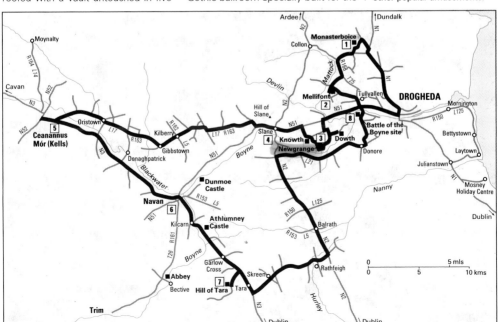

visit of George IV in 1821. Lady Conyngham is said to have been the King's mistress, and his writing desk can be seen in the drawing room. The castle's situation makes it a dramatic venue for open-air pop concerts. The Rolling Stones, Bruce Springsteen, U2 and David Bowie have attracted hundreds of thousands to this narrow valley.

*The Bronze Age tomb at Newgrange. At the winter solstice, the sun's rays shine down the passageway inside, illuminating the burial chamber*

> *Take the **N51** for Navan, and after a mile (2km) turn right on to the **R163 (L17)** for Kells*

## Kells, Co Meath

**5** Kells, or Ceanannus Mór, was one of the great religious centres of western Europe. You can pick out the circular ditch in the lie of the town, and see the **round tower**, an early **church** and the impressive **Celtic crosses** with their scriptural messages. The town is famous for the Book of Kells, the celebrated illuminated medieval manuscript, now held in Trinity College, Dublin.

> *Take the **N3** for 10 miles (16km) to Navan.*

## Navan, Co Meath

**6** The administrative centre of the county has a self-possessed and prosperous air. Once a walled town, Navan marks the meeting of the waters of the Boyne and the Blackwater. Look out for the stocks outside the town hall, and a very modern blue sculpture, which is dedicated to 'the Fifth Province, the ideal of the cultural integration of all the people of Ireland'. The town has a good race course. Close by are the ruins of **Athlumney Castle, Dunmoe Castle** and **Bective Abbey**.

> *Take the **N3** for Dublin, and after 6 miles (10km) turn right at the signpost for Tara.*

## Tara, Co Meath

**7** The seat of the High Kings of Ireland, the **Hill of Tara** commands majestic views over the fertile plains of Meath and for miles beyond. This was the centre of Ireland's heroic age, a civilisation that had contact with the Roman Empire, and was ruled by a king who was concerned with sacred rites and rituals as well as political matters. A *feis* at royal Tara was a renowned festivity, held at harvest, or for the crowning of a king, of which the dynastic O'Neills were the strongest.

Five chariot roads led here from all parts of Ireland. The **Rath of the Synods** is an elaborate trivallate earthwork. The **Mound of the Hostages**, a Stone Age passage-

*In the past, royalty were entertained at Slane Castle. Now it provides a dramatic setting for open-air rock concerts*

tomb that stands inside the **Royal Enclosure**, is an Iron Age hillfort and encloses the **Royal Seat**, a ringfort. On **Cormac's House** is the **Stone of Destiny**, said to be the inauguration stone of the kings. Also here are the **Banquet Hall**, the **Enclosure of King Laoghaire**, the **Sloping Trenches** and **Grainne's Enclosure**. A statue of St Patrick recalls his profound influence, but it was the coming of Christianity that led to the eventual decline of Tara.

*Return to the **N3** and turn right. After 2 miles (3km) turn left following the signpost to Skreen Church and Cross, go straight over the crossroads, twice, and follow a narrow, uneven road for 4½ miles (7km), then turn left to Drogheda. After a mile (2km) turn left towards Slane on the **N2** for 8 miles (13km) and follow the marked route for the Battle of the Boyne Site.*

## Battle of the Boyne Site, Co Louth and Co Meath

**8** It does not take a great effort of the imagination to picture the field of battle in 1690, when the armies of William of Orange and James II met each other in a conflict that was significant for Ireland, Britain and Europe.

A huge orange and green sign beside the deep waters of the Boyne marks the main site of the conflict, while helpful signs along the way show where the opposing armies camped, where battle was joined and where the river was crossed. The route passes along the **Boyne Navigation Canal**, once a link in a grand scheme to connect Ireland's major rivers.

*Take the **N51** for 4 miles (6km) to Drogheda.*

Drogheda – Monasterboice **6 (10)**
Monasterboice – Mellifont **4 (6)**
Mellifont – Newgrange **9 (14)**
Newgrange – Slane **6 (10)**
Slane – Kells **15 (24)**
Kells – Navan **10 (16)**
Navan – Tara **7 (11)**
Tara – Battle of the Boyne Site **23 (37)**
Battle of the Boyne Site – Drogheda **4 (6)**

---

**RECOMMENDED WALKS**

**8** *Battle of the Boyne Site, Co Louth and Co Meath* At Townley Hall, the Forest and Wildlife Service has developed a waymarked trail that takes the walker close to the site of the Battle of the Boyne, and gives views over the valley. The walk up the wooded banks of the river is steep in places. A trail leaflet is available at the site.

**1/2 days – 89 miles (143km)**

# DUBLIN
# & WICKLOW

**Dublin • Dun Laoghaire • Killiney • Bray • Enniskerry
Roundwood • Glendalough • Poulaphouca • Blessington
The Sally Gap • Killakee • Dublin**

**D**ublin is a busy, self-important and increasingly commercial city, but the arts thrive, it has its own certain style and its people know how to enjoy themselves. Take a walk at dusk around one of the fine Georgian squares, as lights illuminate the first-floor decorated plaster ceilings and note the uniformity of architecture, and the variety of door-knockers, fanlights, foot-scrapers and coal-hole covers. Do a pub crawl, or a park crawl or a church crawl, there is plenty to explore. Don't miss the special ambiance of *Trinity College*, or Dean Swift's (author of *Gulliver's Travels*) *St Patrick's*. Admire Ireland's cultural flowering in a visit to the new *Irish Museum of Modern Art* at the fine old Royal Hospital in Kilmainham, or remember the cultural renaissance of Yeats and Lady Gregory in a visit to the *Abbey Theatre*. At *Phoenix Park*, Europe's largest enclosed park, you can go to the zoo, watch polo or catch a glimpse of the President on her way to her residence.

*Fiddlers at the Cultúrlann in Monkstown, on Dublin Bay. Traditional music has a high profile in Ireland, and can be heard almost everywhere*

*i* 14 Upper O'Connell Street

*Take the **R118 (T44)** for 7 miles (11km) to Dun Laoghaire.*

### Dun Laoghaire, Co Dublin

**1** This is a place to promenade, along the extensive harbour piers, or past the villas on the front, or through the parks. Savour the Victorian features of the place which was called Kingstown from the visit of George IV in 1821 until the establishment of the Irish Free State. When the granite piers were completed in 1859, the harbour was the biggest artificial haven in the world. Large ships use the port and it is the home of several yacht clubs, of which the Royal St George and the Royal Irish are the oldest. In keeping with all of this, Dun Laoghaire has a fine **Maritime Museum**.

Near by, at **Sandycove**, is a **Martello tower**, one of the distinctive squat round coastal defences erected in Napoleonic times. This one houses a **museum** of the writer, James Joyce, who stayed there briefly. The Martello tower and the nearby 'Forty foot' gentlemen's bathing place form a vividly described part of *Ulysses*.

*i* St Michael's Wharf

*Take the **R119 (T44)** coastal road for 5 miles (8km) to Dalkey and Killiney.*

*The broad sweep of Killiney Bay, known as Ireland's Bay of Naples, with Bray Head and the two Sugar Loaf mountains in the distance. The elegant town consists of attractive villas set in tree-filled gardens*

### Killiney, Co Dublin

**2** With the broad sweep of a steeply dropping bay, elegant villas among tree-filled gardens and the two Sugar Loaf mountains to complete the vista, Killiney has been likened to the Bay of Naples. Indeed a good place to gain a full panorama is a place called **Sorrento Point.**

Quite a way inland from the popular beach is **Killiney Hill**, where an attractive park gives superb views from a height of the hills and sea. Its 18th-century stone **obelisk** was built as a famine relief project.

*Continue on the R119 (T44), then join the N11 for 4 miles (6km) to Bray.*

### Bray, Co Wicklow

**3** A popular resort that retains much of its Victorian attraction, Bray's long beach stretches below the strong line of Bray Head, an extension of the Wicklow dome. From the promenade you can walk the outstanding cliff path for 3 miles (5km) to **Greystones.** Below the Head, fan-like fossils of the oldest known Irish animals have been found. In the town is an attractive **Heritage Centre.**

Close by is **Dargle Glen**, a lovely wooded valley set in rugged mountains. **Dargle Glen gardens**, which combine excellent planting with works of art, are occasionally opened to the public by their owner.

**Kilruddery**, by contrast, was one of the great set-piece landscape gardens of the 17th century. Very few of these early formal gardens, designed on a large scale with geometric patterns of water, avenues and plants now survive.

*Return to and take the N11 for Wicklow, then turn left for Enniskerry.*

### Enniskerry, Co Wicklow

**4** The first Irish Roman Catholic Gothic revival church was built in this pretty village in 1843. Its spire is an attractive feature in the lovely glen of **Glencullen.**

The superb mountain setting enhances **Powerscourt**, one of Ireland's great gardens, extravagantly created by the 6th and 7th Viscounts Powerscourt, and extensively altered between 1843 and 1875. A formal landscape of water, terraces, statues, ironwork, plants, flowers and ancient trees is stunningly contrasted with the natural beauty of Sugar Loaf Mountain, combining to form one of the most photographed vistas in the country. The house was a magnificent Palladian mansion, designed by Richard Castle, but was destroyed by fire in 1974. Also in the estate is **Powerscourt waterfall** where the Dargle river torrents over a face 400-feet (120m) high.

*Take the R760 (T43) south, turning left to Killough. Take the R755 (T61) for 8 miles (13km) to Roundwood.*

### Roundwood, Co Wicklow

**5** The highest village in Ireland, Roundwood sits amid lovely scenery. The Vartry Reservoir, which helps to serve Dublin, lies close to the village. To the northeast is the **Glen of the Downs**, a dry rocky gorge formed in the Ice Age, with an oak wood. The landscape gives an idea of what Ireland would have looked like in pre-

## RECOMMENDED WALKS

The **Wicklow Way** is a long-distance walk that follows a course from Marley Park in the north to Shillelagh and then through into County Carlow, on high ground on the east of the Dublin and Wicklow Mountains. The route is mostly way-marked through forests, along old bog roads and up steep mountain tracks. It is best to come equipped for wet weather and wear strong walking shoes. In addition, there are dozens of forest walks through Wicklow.

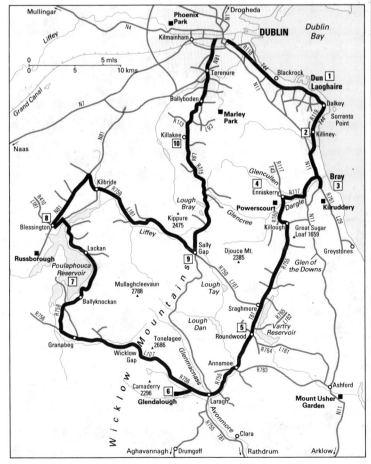

## SCENIC ROUTES

The road from Sally Gap to Laragh rises and falls wonderfully, with views across the **Cloghoge Valley** to **War Hill**. The road goes south through rugged mountain land, into forest plantations and passes **Glenmacnass**, a deep glen formed by glaciers, with a magnificent waterfall.

*The Round Tower, set in beautiful Glendalough, the 'Glen of Two Lakes'*

historic times, before the clearance of the forests. Lough Dan and Lough Tay are dark loughs shadowed by granite.

Six miles (10km) southeast of Roundwood at Ashford is **Mount Usher**, one of the finest examples of the 'Wild Garden', an idea particularly suited to Irish gardens. In a sheltered valley, plants, which include many exotic species, grow naturally and in abundance in perfect harmony with the gentle landscape. They spread along the banks of a winding stream with cascades that are spanned by unusual suspension bridges.

*Continue on the **R755 (T61)** for 5 miles (8km) to Laragh, then turn right on to the **R756 (L107)** for 1 mile (2km) to Glendalough.*

### FOR CHILDREN

**6** *Glendalough, Co Wicklow*
Children may like to see **Clara**, the smallest village in Ireland, which contains two houses, a church and a school. Clara lies in a beautiful valley southeast of Glendalough. They will also enjoy the **Clara Lara Funpark** on the banks of the Avonmore river, which has boating, an adventure playground, picnic and barbecue sites and fishing on a trout farm.

### Glendalough, Co Wicklow

**6** Glendalough, the glen of two loughs, is the loveliest and most historic of all its Wicklow rivals. Two beautiful loughs lie deep in a valley of granite escarpments and rocky outcrops. On its green slopes are the gentle contours of native trees, on its ridges the jagged outline of pines. Add to this picturesque scene a soaring round tower, and ruined stone churches spreading through the valley and you have a combination which makes Glendalough one of the most beautiful and historic places in Ireland. St Kevin came to Glendalough in the 6th century to escape worldly pleasures. He lived as a hermit, in a cell on a little shelf above the lake, but the settlement he founded flourished and grew to become a monastic city whose influence spread throughout Europe. The **round tower** was built when Viking raids troubled the

*Mount Usher Gardens and House at Ashford. The gardens were originally laid out in 1860 by Edmund Walpole*

serenity of Glendalough. Some of the little churches have fine stone carvings, and one has a good pitched stone roof. Guides will explain the full story of Glendalough, and a **Visitor Centre** skilfully illustrates the life of a monastery.

To the south near **Rathdrum** is **Avondale**, the home of the great Irish leader Charles Stewart Parnell. The 18th-century house, now a museum, is set in a large beautiful forest park on the banks of the Avonmore river.

*Follow the **R756 (L107)** through the Wicklow Gap for 11 miles (18km), then turn right on to the **R758** for Poulaphouca.*

### Poulaphouca, Co Wicklow

**7** At Poulaphouca there are large lakes, now dammed to supply Dublin's water system and also forming part of the Liffey hydroelectric scheme. The proximity to the city and the abundance of lakeside roads, makes it a popular venue for Dubliners.

*Follow the lakeside road by Lackan for 10 miles (16km) to Blessington.*

### Blessington, Co Wicklow

**8** An attractive village with a long main street, Blessington was an important coaching stop on the main road south from Dublin.

Just south is **Russborough House**, serenely placed in a beautiful landscape before a fine lake. It was built in the middle of the 18th century, the work of architect Richard Castle, for Joseph Leeson, the Earl of Milltown. A Palladian house, constructed of granite, it sweeps out elegantly along curving colonnades to flanking wings and pavilions. Decorative features include superb plasterwork by the Francini brothers, and the house now contains the famous **Beit Art Collection**.

*Take the **N81** for Dublin. After 4½ miles (7km) turn right on to the **R759 (L161)** to The Sally Gap.*

### The Sally Gap, Co Wicklow

**9** The most complete stretch of blanket bog on the east of the country is the beautiful Sally Gap. There are many pools and streams here, and the characteristic bog plant, the bog rosemary.

*Turn sharp left on to the **R115 (L94)** for 9 miles (14km) to Killakee.*

### Killakee, Co Dublin

**10** The view from Killakee gives an outstanding picture of Dublin, as George Moore put it 'wandering between the hills and the sea'. It shows the impressive crescent of Dublin Bay, bounded by the twin bastions of Howth Head to the north and Killiney Head to the south. The River Liffey is clearly defined, and you can identify the green landmark of Phoenix Park.

South of Killakee is a **tower**, the eerie remains of a retreat of the **Hell Fire Club**, formed by a group of rakes in 1735. There were terrible tales of their wickedness, the worst involving a game of cards with the devil.

North of Killakee, towards Dublin, is **Marley Park**, an attractive parkland that combines river, wood, miniature railway and craft centre. In the same area is **St Enda's Park**, which contains the house where Patrick Pearse, one of the revolutionary leaders in 1916, had his school. The house is now a Pearse Museum.

*Follow the **R115 (L94)** for 7 miles (11km) back to Dublin.*

## FOR HISTORY BUFFS

**7** *Poulaphouca, Co Wicklow* At **Derrynamuck**, south of Poulaphouca, is the **Dwyer Cottage**, where Michael Dwyer, a leader in 1798, was trapped by the British. He escaped because of the heroic action of Samuel McAllister who drew the fire at the critical time.

**9** *The Sally Gap, Co Wicklow* Wicklowmen played a large part in the 1798 rebellion, and in order to suppress the uprising finally and clear the mountains, the '**Military Road**' was forged from Rathfarnham in the north through The Sally Gap to Aghavannagh in the south. Former barracks can be seen at Drumgoff and Aghavannagh.

## BACK TO NATURE

The wide open spaces of the Wicklow Mountains offer opportunities for seeing a variety of upland birds, including peregrines, merlins, hen harriers, ring ousels and red grouse. In the glens, wood warblers and the occasional redstart may be seen.

**2/3 days – 201 miles (324km)**

# WITCHES, CASTLES & HORSES

Kilkenny ● Thomastown ● New Ross ● Carlow ● Kildare
Port Laoise ● Abbeyleix ● Thurles ● Cashel
Fethard ● Kilkenny

Kilkenny is a thriving, prosperous town with much of its history still housed in original structures and one of the most highly regarded craft centres in Ireland. *St Canice's Cathedral* (Church of Ireland), which dates from the 13th century, is thought to occupy the site of the saint's original 6th-century church off Dean Street. *Kilkenny Castle*, built in 1391, is set on high ground above the river, and retains the lines of a medieval fortress, with three of its four original corner towers intact. The *Rothe House* in Parliament Street was built in 1594 as the home of a prosperous Tudor merchant. It now houses the *Kilkenny Archaeological Society Museum and Library* which displays fascinating relics of historical and cultural significance.

Other fine buildings include *Shee's Almshouse* in Rose Street and *The Tholsel* in High Street. *Kilkenny Design Centre*, located in old stables and coach houses across from the castle, is home to first-rate designers and craftspeople who produce outstanding contemporary and classic designs in textiles, ceramics, glassware, jewellery and metals.

*An ancient dolmen, dating from 2000BC, at Browne's Hill Demesne, near Carlow. The giant capstone, the largest in Ireland, weighs 100 tons (101 tonnes)*

ℹ️ Rose Inn Street

*Take the R700 (T20) southeast for 11 miles (18km) to Thomastown.*

### Thomastown, Co Kilkenny

**1** This prosperous little market town on the banks of the River Nore is named after Thomas FitzAnthony Walsh, Seneschal of Leinster, who built a castle and walled the town in the early 13th century. **Grennan Castle**, about 1½ miles (2km) to the southwest, fell to Cromwell in 1650 and is now in ruins. The most impressive remains of ancient buildings in the town are those of a large 13th-century church.

**Jerpoint Cistercian Abbey**, 2 miles (3km) southwest of Thomastown on the **N9**, is one of Ireland's finest monastic ruins. Founded in the 12th century, it was dissolved and its lands given to the Ormonde family in 1540. The extensive remains are awe-inspiring, with the original Romanesque pillars, a fine chancel and the most decorative cloister arcade of any Irish church. The detailed secular and religious carved figures are an accurate portrayal of the armour and clothing of 15th- and 16th-century Ireland. A **Visitor Centre** provides information on the abbey's long history.

**Mount Juliet**, signposted from the town centre, was once one of Ireland's largest private estates, covering 1,411 acres (570 hectares) of

*The Irish National Stud, at Tully, on the outskirts of Kildare, where many champion racehorses have been bred and trained. The stud also incorporates a museum and is an important centre for equine research*

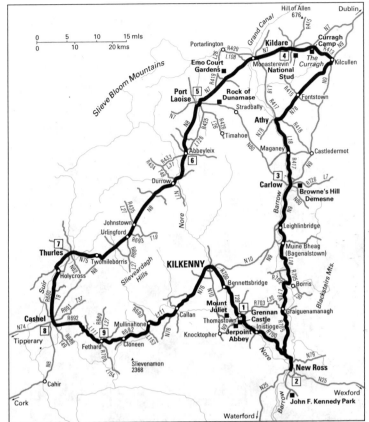

## RECOMMENDED WALKS

1 *Thomastown, Co Kilkenny*
Walk along the banks of the River Nore for 1½ miles (2km) to the southwest to reach the remains of 13th-century **Grennan Castle**. The river walk is wooded, with patches of rich pasture, and the lawn between the castle ruins and the river is covered with daffodils in spring.

3 *Carlow, Co Carlow* There is a pleasant walk in Carlow town along the banks of the River Barrow to the junction with its Burrin tributary. The meeting of the two rivers forms an attractive four-angled lake.

## SPECIAL TO ...

*Kilkenny, Co Kilkenny*
Kilkenny was the home of Ireland's most famous witches. In 1324 Dame Alice Kyteler was the owner of Kyteler's Inn in St Kieran's Street. A beautiful woman who had become wealthy following the successive deaths of her four husbands, she was accused of witchcraft and condemned to a public whipping, followed by burning at the stake. She escaped, leaving her maid to be burnt in her place and was never seen again. She is said to haunt the house still.

## BACK TO NATURE

2 *New Ross Co Wexford*
About 6 miles (10km) south of New Ross, signposted from the **N25** east, is the 480-acre (195-hectare) **John F Kennedy Park and Arboretum**, the Irish government's tribute to the American president (1961-3) whose ancestral home is in nearby **Dunganstown**. Nearly 300 acres (120 hectares) are given over to an arboretum that holds more than 5,000 shrubs and trees from all over the world. Follow the signposts to the top of **Slieve Coillte** for a panoramic view of south Wexford and the splendid estuary of the rivers Barrow, Nore and Suir.

woodlands, pastures and landscaped lawns. Now a luxury hotel, the grounds provide an exceptionally beautiful drive off the main roads, and its public rooms are open to non-guests.

*Take the **R700 (T20)** southeast for 14 miles (23km) to Mountgarret Bridge, where it joins the **N79** for the short drive to New Ross.*

### New Ross, Co Wexford

2 There is much of its medieval beginnings in the narrow streets lined with tall, buildings that climb the steep hill on which New Ross is built, overlooking the River Barrow. The town invites exploration by foot, and many of the streets are stepped and inaccessible to vehicles. The long bridge in the town centre connects New Ross to County Kilkenny on the opposite side. The first bridge was built around 1200 and the town was soon walled. In 1643, it held off a siege by the Duke of Ormonde, but fell to Cromwell just six years later. It was captured and then lost by insurgents in 1798, leaving the town in flames and many of its inhabitants slain.

The **Tholsel** (Town Hall) had to be rebuilt in 1806 when the original 18th-century structure fell victim to subsidence. It has a fine clock tower and holds the maces of Edward III and Charles II and ancient volumes of the minutes of the old town corporation. The 1798 memorial at the Tholsel depicts a 'croppy boy', typical of the insurgents who assaulted the town.

River cruises depart from the Quay during the summer months, with lunch and dinner sailings. (See also Tour 15.)

*Head north on the **N79**, turn left on to the **R700 (T20)**, then right after a short distance on to the **R705 (L18A)** for 23 miles (37km) to join the **N9** at Leighlinbridge for the 7-mile (11km) drive into Carlow.*

### Carlow, Co Carlow

3 The little village of Graiguenamanagh ('the granary of the monks'), between New Ross and Carlow, was once a place of great ecclesiastical importance. Occupying the site was the **Abbey of Duiske**, built between 1207 and 1240. It was suppressed in 1536, but determined monks stayed on for many years afterwards before abandoning the extensive settlement. By 1774 it stood in ruins and the tower collapsed. A large part of the church was roofed[*] in 1813 and Catholic services were resumed. In the 1970s, a group of dedicated locals undertook a major restoration, and today the completely restored abbey serves as the parish church.

The county town of Ireland's second smallest county, Carlow was an Anglo-Norman stronghold, strategically placed on the border of the English 'Pale', a protected area around Dublin and its environs. The 640 insurgents who fell here during their 1798 attack on the town are remembered by a fine Celtic cross.

The west wall and the two flanking towers of 13th-century **Carlow Castle** can be seen near the bridge across the Barrow. This Norman castle was destroyed not by Cromwell, who captured it in 1650, but by one Dr Middleton in 1814 when his zeal to convert it into an insane asylum led him to try to reduce the thickness of the walls with explosives, leaving it a dangerous shell, most of which had to be demolished for safety reasons.

The **Cathedral of the Assumption**, in Tullow Street, is a fine Gothic-style building erected between 1828 and 1833. Of special interest are its 151-foot (46m) high lantern tower and the marble monument, by the sculptor John Hogan, of the 19th-century political writer, Bishop Doyle.

Adjacent to the town hall and housed in an old theatre, the **Haymarket Museum** contains a reconstructed forge and kitchen as well as military relics and local carpentry and coopering tools.

**Browne's Hill Demesne**, about 2 miles (3km) east of town, holds a mammoth dolmen, whose capstone is the largest in Ireland.

*Follow the R417 (L18) north for 12 miles (19km) to Athy. Turn northeast on to the N78 for 14 miles (23km) to Kilcullen, then northwest on the R413 (L19) to its junction with the N7, which takes you west to Kildare.*

*The Japanese Gardens at Kildare are considered by many to be the finest in Europe*

### Kildare, Co Kildare

**4** En route to Kildare, stop in **Athy** to view the **Dominican church**, whose fan-shaped design is a striking example of modern church architecture. Inside are outstanding **Stations of the Cross** by George Campbell and interesting stained glass windows. A 9-mile (14km) detour southeast of Athy on the R418 will take you to **Castledermot**, whose ecclesiastical ruins include a round tower, two high crosses and the remains of a Franciscan friary church.

In the heart of Ireland's horse breeding and training industry, Kildare sits on the edge of the vast Curragh plain. The beautiful 18th-century Church of Ireland **St Brigid's Cathedral** incorporates part of a 13th-century church.

East of town, horse racing has reigned supreme for centuries at **The Curragh**, headquarters for the sport in Ireland. Of the several meets held here each year, by far the most famous is the **Irish Sweeps Derby** in June. The **Curragh Camp**, handed over to the Irish army in 1922, has been an important military station for a century, and there you can see the famous 1920 armoured car 'Slievenamon' that carried Michael Collins to the fatal ambush in 1922.

The **Hill of Allen**, legendary home of Irish folk hero Fionn MacCumhail (Finn MacCool) and the site of three royal residences in ancient Leinster, is 8 miles (13km) northeast of town via the **R415 (L180)**. It rises from the surrounding plain, and is crowned by a battlemented stone tower built in the 19th century from which there are magnificent views.

*Take the **N7** southwest for 20 miles (32km) to reach Port Laoise.*

### Port Laoise, Co Laois

**5** Set at the junction of the Dublin/ Limerick and Dublin/Cork main roads, Port Laoise is also the site of Ireland's national prison. A less grim feature of the town is the collection of antique cars and other forms of transport in the veteran **Car Museum**.

There is a well preserved 12th-century **round tower** in the little village of **Timahoe**, about 7 miles (11km) southeast of Port Laoise via the **R426 (L26)**. Four miles (6km) east of town, the **Rock of Dunamase** rises 200 feet (60m) above the plain, with the ruined 12th-century **castle** of Dermot MacMurrough, the king of Leinster.

**Emo Court Gardens**, about 8 miles (13km) northeast of Port Laoise off the **N7**, are probably the premier attraction of County Laois. The grand house was designed by the celebrated architect James Gandon. It is open only to special interest groups, but the grounds are open to all and contain an imposing lake and hundreds of specimen trees, shrubs, and flowering plants.

To the west of town, the many roads crossing the Slieve Bloom Mountains offer interesting and scenic drives.

*Take the **N8** for 9 miles (14km) south to Abbeyleix.*

---

*Kilkenny Castle, a blend of Gothic and classical styles, is situated on the high bank of the River Nore and is surrounded by gardens. It was once the principal seat of the Butler family, Earls and Dukes of Ormonde*

### SCENIC ROUTES

Leaving Thomastown by the **R703 (L32)** east, the 8-mile (13km) drive to **Graiguenamanagh** provides tremendous views of the River Barrow and the long ridge of the **Blackstairs Mountains** and 1,694-foot (516m) **Brandon Hill** to the south.

The Carlow/Stradbally road **(N8)** takes you through Windy Gap, one of eastern Ireland's most famous scenic drives, with wide vistas of the surrounding countryside.

## Abbeyleix, Co Laois

**6** This attractive town, with tree-lined streets, is noted for the de Vesci Demesne, known as **Abbeyleix House**. The great house, which dates back to 1773, is not open to the public, but the splendid grounds which include formal terrace gardens to the west of the house, a 'wild garden' (called the Paradise Garden) that is carpeted with bluebells in spring, an American garden with magnolia trees, and a magnificent avenue of lime trees are.

*Take the **N8** for 24 miles (39km) southwest to the **N75** turnoff that leads to Thurles.*

## Thurles, Co Tipperary

**7** In ancient times, the O'Fogartys fortified this site on the River Suir, and although the Norman Strongbow's army was soundly defeated here in 1174, Anglo-Normans returned later to build a castle that would protect the crossing. Today it is a busy, well laid out marketing centre for the surrounding agricultural area. It is also the cathedral town of the archdiocese of Cashel and Emly.

*Take the **R660 (T9)** south for 13 miles (21km) to reach Cashel.*

## Cashel, Co Tipperary

**8** Look above the ground floor of the shop opposite the city hall to see the crenellated battlements and gargoyles of what was the 15th-century Quirke's Castle, named after a family who lived there in the 19th century. At the southwest end of Main Street, the ornamental fountain is in memory of

*Abbeyleix House, home of the de Vesci's. This English family lost much of its power for 'over-promoting' the Irish cause*

Dean Kinane and his efforts in bringing an extension of the railway to Cashel in 1904. (See Tours 3 and 10.)

*Take the **R692 (L111)** for 10 miles (16km) southeast to Fethard.*

## Fethard, Co Tipperary

**9** This small town was an important Anglo-Norman settlement in medieval times. Remnants of the old town walls and their flanking towers can still be seen. Right in the town centre, there are keeps of three 15th-century castles, including that of **Fethard Castle**. Well-preserved remains of an ancient priory contain several 16th- and 17th-century tombs. More than a thousand exhibits of rural life in this area are on display at the interesting **Folk, Farm and Transport Museum**.

*Take the **R692 (L111)** northeast for 11 miles (18km) to Mullinahone. Turn right for Callan, then north on joining the **N76** for the 11-mile (18km) drive back to Kilkenny.*

| | |
|---|---|
| Kilkenny – Thomastown | **11 (18)** |
| Thomastown – New Ross | **16 (26)** |
| New Ross – Carlow | **34 (55)** |
| Carlow – Kildare | **34 (55)** |
| Kildare – Port Laoise | **20 (32)** |
| Port Laoise – Abbeyleix | **9 (14)** |
| Abbeyleix – Thurles | **30 (48)** |
| Thurles – Cashel | **13 (21)** |
| Cashel – Fethard | **10 (16)** |
| Fethard – Kilkenny | **24 (39)** |

**FOR HISTORY BUFFS**

**9** *Fethard, Co Tipperary* The ancient name for **Slievenamon**, just southeast of Fethard, was 'The Mountain of the Women of Feimhinn' in honour of the fairy women of the area who, according to legend, enchanted Fionn and his Fianna warriors. It is also believed that it was here that Fionn decreed he would take as his bride the first woman to reach him in a race to the summit. The winner was Grainne, who created a legend of her own when she later opted for Diarmuid as a mate.

3 days – 163 miles (262km)

*A master cutter at work on a large crystal vase at the Waterford Crystal glassworks. The design is cut strictly from memory and requires immense skill and dexterity*

# BY HOOK OR BY CROOKE

Wexford • Courtown • Gorey • Enniscorthy • New Ross
Waterford • Passage East • Ballyhack • Hook Head
Fethard • Kilmore Quay • Lady's Island • Rosslare • Wexford

[i] Crescent Quay

*Take the **R741 (L29)** north, then turn right on to the **R742 (L30A)** for the 25-mile (40km) drive to Courtown.*

## Courtown, Co Wexford

**1** This pleasant little harbour town set in the wide sweep of Courtown Bay is a popular family resort, with a fine, 2-mile (3km) long sandy beach, amusements and a picturesque golf course. Its harbour piers were a part of famine relief work sponsored by the Earl of Courtown in 1847.

Ballymoney, a small holiday resort with an excellent beach, is 3 miles (5km) north of Courtown, and to the south, **Ardamine** and **Pollshone** are secluded coves with good swimming. At Ardamine, look for the little **church** by George Edmund Street, designer of the London Law Courts and restorer of Christ Church Cathedral in Dublin.

*Follow the **R742 (L31)** for 4 miles (6km) northwest to Gorey.*

## Gorey, Co Wexford

**2** Set against a backdrop of the Wicklow Mountains to the north, Gorey dates back to the 13th century. The wide Main Street and neat street plan give it a pleasant appearance. It figured prominently in the 1798

*The battlemented and ivy-clad façade at Waterford Castle*

A Viking town founded in the mid-19th century on the River Slaney, Wexford retains much of the old Norse layout, with tiny lanes leading down to the river. The narrow main street, pedestrianised during certain hours, is lined with traditional shopfronts and pubs, and is the shopping centre of this lively, prosperous little town in which industry, agriculture and tourism form a happy relaxed blend.

The *Bull Ring*, a wide intersection at the north end of Main Street that was the venue for bull baiting in medieval times, is centred by a bronze statue of a pikeman, symbolic of the poorly armed peasantry who defended the town in the rebellion of 1798.

## RECOMMENDED WALKS

**2** *Gorey, Co Wexford* Three miles (5km) northeast of Gorey, on an unclassified, signposted road to Castletown, **Tara Hill** rises to a height of 833 feet (254m). There are lovely forest walks, and the view from the summit is spectacular.

**3** *Enniscorthy, Co Wexford* At **Dunanore Bridge**, 3 miles (5km) south of Enniscorthy, **Dunanore Forest Park** is reached via an unclassified road to Killurin on the west side of the River Slaney. It is an ideal place for a picnic, with beautiful forest and riverside walks.

## FOR CHILDREN

*Wexford, Co Wexford* The **Irish National Heritage Park**, some 3 miles (5km) northeast of Wexford, via the **N25**, has authentic reconstructions of Irish life including a campsite, farmstead and portal dolmen from the Stone Age; a stone circle from the Bronze Age; an ogham stone, ringfort and souterrain, Viking boathouse and crannóg from the Celtic and early Christian ages; and a Norman motte and bailey, the first Norman fortification in Ireland and a round tower from the early Norman period. There is also a fine nature walk.

conflict, and insurgents camped at the western end of town at 418-foot (127m) high **Gorey Hill** before they marched on Arklow. A granite Celtic cross stands near the hill as a memorial to those who fell in battle. The **Loreto convent**, designed by Pugin, dates from 1839 to 1842.

*Take the N11 for 19 miles (31km) southwest to Enniscorthy.*

## Enniscorthy, Co Wexford

**3** Set on the steeply sloping banks of the River Slaney, Enniscorthy suffered several attacks following the arrival of the Normans, and it was a veritable storm centre of the 1798 rebellion, when insurgents led by the revered Father John Murphy held the town for four weeks before being overthrown by Crown forces under General Lake. A bronze statue of Father Murphy and a pikeman stands in Market Square. The battles of 1916 are commemorated by a memorial to Commandant Seamus Rafter that stands in **Abbey Square**.

**St Aidan's Cathedral** is an impressive Gothic-revival structure designed by Pugin for the commanding site overlooking the river. Housed in a Norman castle, **Enniscorthy County Museum** displays mementoes of both the 1798 and 1916 uprisings, as well as a host of items that figured in the lives of Irish country people of the past. One of its most interesting exhibits is a country 'still' in such good condition it is capable of producing Ireland's illegal alcoholic 'poteen' (pronounced *potcheen*). It is said that

the poet Spenser wrote some of his epic *Faerie Queene* while living in the castle.

The 390-foot (120m) high **Vinegar Hill** at the eastern edge of town is where the Wexford pikemen made their last stand in June 1798. Their defeat marked the end of any effective resistance in the county. Today, it is a peaceful vantage point from which to view the town and the surrounding countryside.

*Follow the N79 southwest for 21 miles (34km) to reach New Ross.*

## New Ross, Co Wexford

**4** The busy port town of New Ross was founded by Isabella, granddaughter of the Irish king, Dermot MacMurrough, and daughter of the Norman leader Strongbow. The River Barrow that runs through the town links up with Ireland's inland waterway system.

**Old Ross**, a tiny village 5 miles (8km) east of town lost its importance in ancient times with the development and growth of New Ross.

Eight miles (13km) south of New Ross via the **R733 (L159)**, the ruins of **Dunbrody Abbey**, founded in 1182, are near the little village of **Campile**. They are among the finest in Ireland, with a well preserved nave, aisles, choir and transepts. Each transept is joined by three vaulted and groined chapels. (See also Tour 14.)

*Take the N25 southwest for 15 miles (24km) to Waterford.*

## Waterford, Co Waterford

**5** The most important seaport in the southeast, Waterford's face is lined with traces of its past. The **French Church** in Greyfriars Street was built in 1240 for the Franciscan order, but the extensive ruins serve as a poignant reminder of the Huguenot refugees who fled religious persecution in France in the 17th century and were given use of the church, which had fallen into disuse. Near the City Hall, **St Olaf's Church** dates from the 11th century. The impressive Church of Ireland **Christ Church Cathedral** sits on the elevated site one street off the Quay that once held a Viking church built in 1050. The original structure was replaced in 1773 and the present building has been enlarged and undergone several renovations.

Waterford's lively cultural scene includes the **Waterford Arts Centre** in O'Connell Street, which has permanent and visiting exhibitions, and the **Garter Lane Arts Centre**, also in O'Connell Street, is the venue for special events and exhibitions. (See also Tour 10.)

*The harbour at the little village of Passage East*

*From Waterford take the **R683** **(L157)** east for 7 miles (11km) to Passage East.*

## Passage East, Co Waterford

**6** This picturesque village at the foot of the steep hill overlooking the Waterford harbour estuary was fortified in years gone by to control shipping on the river. These days, it is the County Waterford terminal for the car ferry across to County Wexford. (See also Tour 10.)

*Take the passenger ferry from Passage East across the estuary to Ballyhack.*

## Ballyhack, Co Waterford

**7** The ruined **castle** overlooking the estuary was part of the Preceptory of the Knights of St John, founded in the 11th century. Today, it is the County Wexford terminal for the car ferry from County Waterford and is noted both for salmon fishing and its long tradition of boat building.

SPECIAL TO ...

*Wexford, Co Wexford* The **Wexford Opera Festival** is a gala October/November event of music and festivity, featuring local and international opera companies presenting lesser-known operas as well as standard classics. There are three performances during each week, along with music recitals, workshops, art exhibitions, and many other related activities. Throughout the town, there are peripheral events such as pub singing competitions and street performances.

**3** *Enniscorthy, Co Wexford* In late June/early July, Enniscorthy celebrates the Wexford Strawberry Fair, with tons of the luscious, locally grown fruit and non-stop street entertainment, art exhibitions and musical events.

## FOR HISTORY BUFFS

**8 Hook Head, Co Waterford**
Hook Head gave to the English language one of its most frequently used expressions when the Norman leader Strongbow, Earl of Pembroke, declared in 1170 that 'I will take Waterford by Hook or by Crooke'. He was referring to the Tower of Hook on the Wexford side and to Crooke Castle on the Waterford shore near Passage East, both of which were heavily fortified. Strongbow made good his vow and thus changed the course of Irish history.

*Turn southeast from Ballyhack on to the **R733 (L159)**, then just past Arthurstown turn right for Duncannon, shortly after which turn on to an unclassified signposted road south for about 7 miles (11km) to Hook Head.*

### Hook Head, Co Waterford

**8** Perched on a craggy sea-carved peninsula, the striking black-and-white lighthouse called the **Tower of Hook** is thought to date from the 12th century. The tradition of a light to guide ships through the treacherous waters of this dangerous point began long before then, however. Legend has it that it was the Welsh monk, St Dubhann, who first tended a cauldron of burning pitch, which he hoisted to the top of a high platform each night. The practice continued right through the 10th to 12th centuries as first the Vikings and then the Normans occupied the Hook area. Raymond le Gros, an important Norman leader, is believed to have built the tower some 800 years ago on the site of the beacon of St Dubhann, and it was this

*A thatched windmill, one of only two intact windmills in Ireland, at Tacumshane, near the picturesque little village of Kilmore Quay. The area is known for its seafood and deep-sea fishing*

structure that was renovated in 1677, when an oil lamp was installed. Nowadays, the lamp is electrically powered with a standby generator, a flashing light and a powerful fog horn. While special permission must be obtained to visit the **lighthouse**, the drive along the peninsula is spectacular, with secluded beaches and coves.

*Return north on the unclassified road for about 4 miles (6km) to the point where it branches off on to another unclassified road to the right, which leads to Fethard.*

### Fethard, Co Wexford

**9** This pleasant little resort on the eastern shore of the Hook Peninsula has a fine sandy beach. In ancient times, there was woodland here, and traces of fossilised tree trunks have been found buried in the sands. The monument in the village centre is in memory of nine members of the Fethard lifeboat crew who drowned in 1914 as they made a gallant attempt to save the crew of a Norwegian vessel that had gone aground.

Fethard Castle, now in ruins but with its round tower still intact, was built in the mid-14th century. Tintern Abbey, 3½ miles (6km) north of Fethard between Wellington Bridge and Duncannon, dates from about

*The county town of Wexford is full of Irish charm. Its narrow main streets contain a lively mix of shops and pubs that are best explored by foot*

1200 and was built by the Earl of Pembroke in thanksgiving for having survived a fierce storm at sea. The long drive into the wooded estate is signposted at the gate. In 1540, following the dissolution of the monasteries, the land and buildings passed into private hands, and parts of the church and tower were used as a residence until 1963. The domestic alterations have now been removed.

*Take the **R734 (L159A)** north for about 4 miles (6km), then turn east on the **R733 (L159)** to Wellington Bridge. Turn right on to the **R736 (L128A)** to Duncormick, then right again via unclassified roads to Kilmore Quay.*

## Kilmore Quay, Co Wexford

**10** The charming little fishing village of Kilmore Quay is noted for its lobsters and deep-sea fishing, and is also the port of departure for the Saltee Islands to the south.

Between the Quay and the village of Kilmore, look for **Brandy Close** and the mound of wooden crosses at the roadside – tradition decrees that mourners place a small cross on the heap each time a funeral passes. The outstanding feature of the village of Kilmore, further along, is its concentration of fine thatched cottages.

*Take the **R739 (L29)** northeast, through Kilmore, to the junction with the **R736**. Turn right on to this road and proceed to its junction with a signposted unclassified road south (at Twelveacre) to Lady's Island.*

## Lady's Island, Co Wexford

**11** Lady's Island is at the head of a saltwater lagoon, Lady's Island Lake. Its ancient name translates to 'Meadow of the Women', and it may well have been inhabited by druidesses. With the coming of Christianity, it became one of the first shrines of the Blessed Virgin and an important place of pilgrimage. The church was destroyed and the holy men of the island were savagely butchered by Cromwellian forces in 1649, but pilgrimages began again at the end of the Cromwellian era and continue to this day.

*Return to Twelveacre via the unclassified road north, then turn northeast on to the **R736** to its junction with the **N25**. Turn right to reach Rosslare Harbour, and straight across to reach Rosslare.*

## Rosslare, Co Wexford

**12** Car and passenger ferries arrive daily at Rosslare Harbour, plying the waters between Wales and northern France. Five miles (8km) to the north, Rosslare is a popular seaside resort with a fine 6-mile (10km) curving beach and good restaurants and accommodation.

*From Rosslare take the **R740** to the **N25** and turn right for 10 miles (16km) to return to Wexford.*

| | |
|---|---|
| Wexford – Courtown | 25 (40) |
| Courtown – Gorey | 4 (6) |
| Gorey – Enniscorthy | 19 (31) |
| Enniscorthy – New Ross | 21 (34) |
| New Ross – Waterford | 15 (24) |
| Waterford – Passage East | 7 (11) |
| Passage East – Ballyhack | ferry |
| Ballyhack – Hook Head | 11 (18) |
| Hook Head – Fethard | 7 (11) |
| Fethard – Kilmore Quay | 24 (39) |
| Kilmore Quay – Lady's Island | 13 (21) |
| Lady's Island – Rosslare | 7 (11) |
| Rosslare – Wexford | 10 (16) |

### BACK TO NATURE

**10** *Kilmore Quay, Co Wexford* The **Saltee Islands**, 4 miles (6km) offshore from Kilmore Quay, harbour huge seabird colonies including razorbills, kittiwakes, puffins and thousands of gulls. Negotiate with local boatmen for the trip out, or arrange for one of the fishing trawlers to drop you on its way out to sea and pick you up on its return.

**11** *Lady's Island, Co Wexford* Lady's Island Lake is itself an important habitat for many bird species. However, on the lake's two islands all five species of terns have established the largest breeding colonies of these birds in Ireland. It is also the only known site at which all species breed together. The islands and terns are easily viewed from the pathway around Lady's Island Lake, but during late spring and summer access to the islands themselves is restricted to prevent disturbance.

### SCENIC ROUTES

The coastal drive via the **R742 (L30A)** from Wexford to Courtown passes through charming little villages, countryside dotted with thatched cottages and stretches of wide sandy beaches.

The road leading southeast out of Ballyhack gives extensive and beautiful views of Waterford harbour estuary as far as Hook Head on the Wexford side and the bulk of Creadan Head on the Waterford side.

# CONNACHT

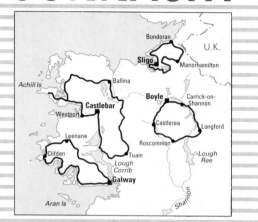

**Tour 16**

This tour, which starts in the bright town of Sligo, is steeped in echoes of Ireland's greatest poet, William Butler Yeats, passing his grave beneath the majestic profile of the mountain, Benbulben, and visiting places which inspired some of his finest lyric poetry. This corner of Ireland is a happy unison of wooded lakes, bare mountain tops and Atlantic seascapes, and abounds in history from prehistoric times.

**Tour 17**

The majestic ruins of its 12th-century abbey and the beauties of its riverside setting and nearby Lough Key Forest Park make Boyle an attractive touring base. The Shannon, with its cruiser-filled marina at Carrick-on-Shannon lures you onward, with perhaps a stop or two along the way for fishing in the

The counties that make up the province of Connacht seem to fit the popular image of Ireland more than any other region. It is a land of stony fields, brooding mountains, windswept cliffs along a rugged coastline dotted with offshore islands, and wide skies alive with the shifting light and shadow of clouds moving inland from the Atlantic.

In the east, County Galway's landscape stretches along flat, fertile plains from Lough Derg and the Shannon Valley north to Roscommon. The streets and lanes of Galway town are filled with medieval architecture and a lively creative arts and crafts culture. Poet William Butler Yeats drew inspiration from the surroundings of his beloved Thor Ballylee tower home near Gort, and Lady Gregory, the moving force behind the Abbey Theatre, gathered some of Ireland's most distinguished writers around her hearth at nearby Coole Park. The three Aran Islands, some 30 miles (48km) offshore, are a repository of antiquities left by prehistoric peoples and the language, customs and dress of a Celtic Twilight heritage. In western Galway, peaks of the Twelve Bens face the misty heights of the Maumturk range across a lake-filled valley in rock-strewn Connemara, whose jagged coastline has a stark, silent beauty punctuated with rocky fields and tiny hamlets.

County Mayo holds reminders of a great prehistoric battle on the plain of Southern Moytura near Cong between the Tuatha De Danann and the Firbolgs. Christianity came with St Patrick, and pilgrims still follow his footsteps to the summit of Croagh Patrick on the shores of island-studded Clew Bay. Achill Island, connected to the mainland by a bridge, is ringed by mighty cliffs and tiny coves, with a flat, boggy interior.

Boyhood visits to his uncle's home in Sligo nurtured W B Yeats' deep love for the west, and some of his best works celebrate Sligo landmarks such as the tiny island of Innisfree and Dooney Rock.

Lough Ree was the haunt of early Christians in County Roscommon, who worshipped in churches and monasteries on many of its islands. Lough Key lies in a luxurious forest park, with the remains of a great abbey at nearby Boyle.

Dominated by inland lakes and the River Shannon, waterlogged County Leitrim has its fair share of mountains and hills. Carrick-on-Shannon, which grew up at one of the traditional fords of the Shannon, is home to a vast flotilla of cabin-cruisers for exploring the river and its lakes.

trout-filled waters of this region. Roscommon's ruined castle speaks of the town's turbulent history, while Clonalis, the 'great house' of Castlerea, is a relic of more gracious times.

## Tour 18

The ghost of Grace O'Malley will follow you on this tour after a visit to magnificent Westport House, with its museum and zoo. After a side trip to her Clare Island home, the route travels to Newport and one of her numerous strongholds before heading for Achill Island, Ireland's largest and most scenic, with yet another castle of the sea queen. At Knock, a huge basilica honouring a miraculous vision of the Blessed Virgin dominates the town. Monastic ruins and impressive Ashford Castle lie along the route as you make your way back to Westport through the county town of Castlebar.

## Tour 19

Galway town's many historic and cultural attractions may tempt you to tarry before setting out on this tour. A trip out to the very special Aran Islands beckons before embarking on the swing through Connemara's starkly beautiful landscape. This Gaeltacht (Irish-speaking) region is one of rocky, untillable fields, where the Twelve Bens mountain range faces the Maumturk range across a lake-filled valley. The jagged coastline is a solitary place of rocks and tiny hamlets and stark, silent beauty.

---

*Quiet fishing villages and distant mountains are typical of the stark and beautiful Connacht landscape. A sense of peace pervades its tranquil seascapes. The area is a stronghold of the Irish languages and customs*

# SLIGO & YEATS COUNTRY

Sligo • Drumcliff • Lissadell • Bundoran • Kinlough
Manorhamilton • Glencar • Lough Gill • Dromahair
Dooney • Strandhill • Sligo

The busy town of Sligo, the largest town in the northwest, has good shops, traditional public houses, thriving art galleries and a theatre. You will remember it for the distinctive backdrop of *Benbulben*, an extraordinary mountain profile, flat-topped and rugged-faced, constantly changing with the light.

The fine ruin of the Dominican *abbey* is mainly 13th-century in origin and the *Church of St John* was remodelled in 1812. The 17th-century *Green Fort* is an earthen structure, while the 18th and 19th century saw fine buildings for Sligo, especially a wonderful Venetian *Court House*. The *County Museum and Art Gallery* reflect the importance of brothers William Butler Yeats, poet and playwright, and Jack B Yeats, artist, both of whom found inspiration in the area. Close to Sligo is *Rosses Point*, a pleasant resort with a championship golf course. The giant statue of a seaman is an unforgettable landmark. Known locally as *'The Metal Man'*, it was erected in 1822 to mark the deep channel of Sligo Bay.

*Roads lead in all directions from Dromahair. The village is in the centre of an historic region, once the territory of the O'Rourke family*

ⓘ Temple Street

*Take the **N15** for 5 miles (8km) to Drumcliff*

### Drumcliff, Co Sligo

**1** *'Under bare Ben Bulben's head*
*In Drumcliff churchyard Yeats is laid*
*An ancestor was rector there*
*Long years ago; a church stands near,*
*By the road an ancient cross,*
*No marble, no conventional phrase;*
*On limestone quarried near the spot,*
*By his command these words are cut:*
*Cast a cold eye*
*On life, on death,*
*Horseman, pass by!'*
Yeats' poem describes Drumcliff completely, and his grave can be found easily in the Protestant churchyard. The main road runs through a monastic site, leaving the stump of a **round tower** on one side of the road, and a 10th-century **high cross** on the other, to the 19th-century **church**, where the poet's grandfather was rector.

*Continue on the **N15** and almost immediately take a turn left for 4 miles (6km) to Lissadell.*

### Lissadell, Co Sligo

**2** The slightly forbidding classical façade of Lissadell hides the romantic background of the Gore-Booths. Yeats was a regular visitor

*Benbulben Mountain is easy to distinguish, even from some distance, because of its very distinctive shape*

here and his poem in memory of the two sisters, Eva and Constance begins:

*'The light of evening, Lissadell,*
*Great windows open to the south,*
*Two girls in silk kimonos, both*
*Beautiful, one a gazelle.'*

Constance became the Countess Markievicz, a leader in the Easter Rising of 1916, and the first woman to be elected to Westminster, although she never took her seat. The 1830s **mansion** is of Ballisodare limestone, and has a charming music room and a dining room with interesting murals. The house is set in fine parkland with small car parks beside the sea, supposedly the warmest bathing water in the country. Seals like it here and can be spotted basking on the sandbanks. On the estate is the Goose Field, where Ireland's largest mainland colony of barnacle geese winter.

*Drive through the parkland to rejoin the road and turn left, then right at the fork. Shortly turn right for Grange and then left, and rejoin the N15 for Bundoran.*

## Bundoran, Co Donegal

**3** Bundoran is a busy seaside resort, and presents quite a contrast to the placid towns and coastal villages of the northwest, offering a wide variety of attractions, as well as a 'blue flag' beach, and cliff walks.

To the southwest at **Streedagh** is a small **park** that commemorates the place where three Armada ships foundered in 1588. Those who struggled ashore from the overladen ships found little succour on land.

*Take the R280 (T54) for 3 miles (5km) to Kinlough.*

## Kinlough, Co Leitrim

**4** Sitting at the north end of **Lough Melvin**, this attractive village is a good place for anglers, with excellent opportunities for coarse and salmon fishing.

The ruins of **Rossclogher Abbey** stand on the shore, and on an artificial island are the remains of the **MacClancy Castle** (known as Rossclogher Castle), where nine survivors of the Armada were given refuge.

*Follow the R281 along the shore of Lough Melvin for 8 miles (13km), then turn right on to the R282 for Manorhamilton, a total distance of 16 miles (26km).*

## Manorhamilton, Co Leitrim

**5** This unassuming village stands in an area of untouched mountain valleys and grey cliff-walls. Lush fertile slopes, steep clefts, and lofty peaks characterise this part of Leitrim. **Glenade Lough** and the valley where the River Bonet rises, have a special quality.

The ruined **castle** that overlooks the town was built at the meeting of four mountain valleys by the Scottish 17th-century planter, Sir Frederick Hamilton, who gave his name to the village.

*Take the N16 for Sligo. After 7 miles (11km) turn right on to an unclassified road for Glencar lake.*

*Rosses Point is a popular yachting and touring centre. W B Yeats often stayed here*

### FOR HISTORY BUFFS

*Sligo, Co Sligo* **Carrowmore**, 2 miles (3km) from Sligo, is the largest group of megalithic tombs in Ireland. Over 60 tombs have been located by archaeologists – the oldest pre-date Newgrange (see Tour 12) by 700 years.

**3** *Bundoran, Co Donegal* **Creevykeel Court Tomb**, southwest of Bundoran, is regarded as the finest example of a classic court tomb in Ireland. The cairn has a kerb of large stones surrounding a ritual court, also with a boundary of upright stones. In the two burial chambers, which were originally roofed, a Harvard archaeological expedition found four cremated burials, as well as decorated neolithic pottery and stone weapons. These are now held in the National Museum in Dublin.

### BACK TO NATURE

**3** *Bundoran, Co Donegal* At **Streedagh**, there is a dune system based on a shingle ridge, which is of international importance, and which supports the plant, insect and bird life associated with dunes. The limestone rocks are laced with varieties of fossil coral. **Bunduff Lake**, near Creevykeel, is a saltwater marsh, where whooper and Bewick swans, Greenland white-fronted geese and many species of duck spend the winter.

## SCENIC ROUTES

**3** *Bundoran, Co Donegal*
From the main Sligo-Donegal road, the **Gleniff Horseshoe** is a signposted loop that passes the jagged summit of **Benwisken** and **Truskmore** mountains.

**10** *Strandhill, Co Sligo* The **Knocknarea** scenic drive gives spectacular views to the south, and to the **Ox mountains** and **Croagh Patrick** in the north.

## FOR CHILDREN

**7** *Lough Gill, Co Leitrim*
Although it was not conceived with children in mind, the **Hazelwood Park** wooden sculptures intrigue and delight them. Along paths in the woods by Lough Gill are huge works of art, hewn, constructed and carved in wood. A walk here is a voyage of discovery, to meet 'Fergus rules the Brazen Car', 'The Old Woman', or 'The Fisherman' among many.

## Glencar, Co Leitrim

**6** Glencar is a beautiful lake, the steep slopes of the valley are generously clothed with mixed woodland, and topped with cliffs. Plants grow here in profusion, including rare species, while the mountain tops are luxuriantly covered with heather. Glencar waterfall cascades down from a rocky headland to a deep pool, white with spray. Yeats immortalised the waterfall in his poem *The Stolen Child*.

*At the end of the lakeside road turn right towards Sligo on the* **N16***, then turn left to Parkes Castle Visitor Centre on the* **R286 (L16)***.*

## Lough Gill, Co Leitrim

**7** From **Parkes Castle** there is a superb view of **Lough Gill**, one of the loveliest loughs imaginable, dotted with islands and wooded with native trees like yew, arbutus, white beam, oak and birch. The bare mountain reaches down deep ferny glens to the lake below.

Parkes Castle is an impressively reconstructed fortified manor house, originally a stronghold of the O'Rourkes, but gaining its present name from the English family who were 'planted' here. An audio-visual show and tea-room will enhance a visit. If you explore the lake shore you will find a sweat-house, medieval Ireland's answer to the sauna.

*Continue on the* **R286 (L16)***, then turn right on to the* **R288 (L112)** *for Dromahair.*

## Dromahair, Co Leitrim

**8** This area is O'Rourke country, overlooked by a rock plateau called O'Rourke's Table. Dromahair enjoys hosting gatherings of the O'Rourke family, as well as a Wild Rose Festival, but it was an English family, the Lane-Foxes, who laid out the pretty village around the River Bonet on a plan based on a Somerset village. In Thomas Moore's song *The Valley lay smiling before me*, the tale is told of the elopement from Dromahair in 1152 of Dervorgilla O'Rourke and the King of Leinster (her husband was away on a pilgrimage of penitence for beating her).

To the west is the Isle of Innisfree. You can take a boat by applying at the house beside the slipway, and see the island for which Yeats yearned – 'where peace comes dropping slow'.

*Take the* **R288 (L112)** *for Carrick-on-Shannon, then turn right on to the* **R287 (L117)** *for Sligo. After 2½ miles (4km) turn right again with the* **R287 (L117)***, and follow the road past the sign for Innisfree to Dooney Rock Forest, before rejoining the* **N4***.*

## Dooney, Co Sligo

**9** This beautiful corner of Lough Gill has forests and paths to satisfy any enthusiastic walker, offering great views of the lough. **Dooney Rock Forest** bears the vestiges of a once important oak forest. You can see the 'twining branches', two linked oaks. Yeats wrote of *'the Fiddler of Dooney'*, who made folk *'dance like the waves of the sea'*. The poem has inspired a **Fiddler of Dooney** competition, for the champion fiddler of Ireland, held in Sligo in July.

**Slish Wood**, or Sleuth Wood as Yeats knew it, has a lovely stream. **Cairns Hill Forest Park** marks the two cairns on Belvoir and Cairns peaks. A legend tells of warriors, Omra and Romra. Romra has a daughter, Gille, meaning beauty, but Omra fell in love

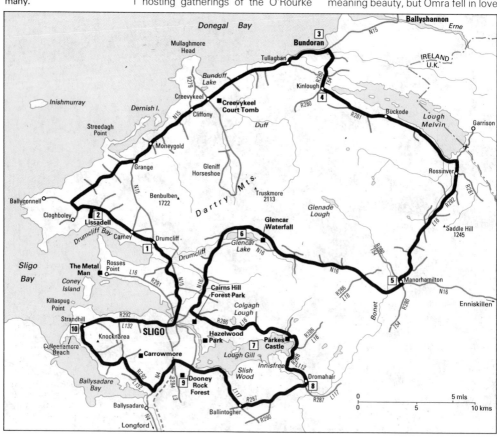

SPECIAL TO...

Sligo and the surrounding district is an important centre of traditional music in Ireland, and in recognition has hosted the **All-Ireland Fleadh**, or festival of traditional music and dancing, in recent years. You will come across music throughout the region, but specialists should visit the **Trades Club** in Castle Street, Sligo. A little further afield, try **The Thatch** in **Ballysadare** or **Killoran's Traditional Restaurant** in **Tobercurry**.

*Glencar waterfall, beside Glencar lake, was immortalised by W B Yeats*

with her. When a mortal battle ensued after the lovers were discovered by Romra, Gille drowned herself, and Lough Gill was formed from the tears of her nursemaid. The legend holds that the two cairns are the burial places of the warriors.

**Cashelore stone fort** is a large oval stone enclosure, once the settlement of an important Celt. The tranquil **Tobernalt** is a **holy well** where mass was said in penal times. A stone altar was erected in thanksgiving when the town was spared the worst ravages of a fever at the turn of the century.

*Travel south on the **N4**, then turn right on to the **R292 (L132)** for Rathcarrick and Strandhill.*

### Strandhill, Co Sligo

**10** Great Atlantic breakers crash on to the beach at Strandhill, making the small seaside village a favoured place for surfing championships. Lifeguards watch bathers, but if you prefer calmer waters, drive round to the beach at **Culleenamore**, which is safer and quiet. Culleenamore nestles under the mountain of **Knocknarea**, which is capped by a **cairn** visible for miles round. It is known locally as the grave of Queen Maeve, the warrior queen of Connacht. If you climb to the summit of Knocknarea, Sligo tradition suggests that you add a stone to the cairn, as a protection against the fairies.

Among the fields below Knocknarea at **Carrowmore** is Ireland's largest group of megalithic tombs; more than 60 can be found here, mostly passage graves and dolmens. The best place to start to discover Carrowmore is from the **Interpretive Centre**, where a map is on display.

*Take the **R292 (L132)** for 5 miles (8km) back to Sligo.*

Sligo – Drumcliff **5 (8)**
Drumcliff – Lissadell **4 (6)**
Lissadell – Bundoran **19 (31)**
Bundoran – Kinlough **3 (5)**
Kinlough – Manorhamilton **16 (26)**
Manorhamilton – Glencar **9 (14)**
Glencar – Lough Gill **15 (24)**
Lough Gill – Dromahair **4 (6)**
Dromahair – Dooney **10 (16)**
Dooney – Strandhill **8 (13)**
Strandhill – Sligo **5 (8)**

### RECOMMENDED WALKS

This is a region well provided with walks, many of them way-marked. Two good town trails can be found in Sligo and Dromahair. There are fine walks from the picnic site beside the village of Kinlough through Kinlough Forest, by Lough Melvin. A spectacular walk takes you from the **Glencar lake** up a mountain road into **Swiss Valley**, a steep-sided cleft, surrounded by peaks. The walk takes you back to the point where the waterfall drops to the lake below.

80

**1 day – 87 miles (140km)**

# BOYLE & THE LAKE COUNTRY

Boyle • Carrick-on-Shannon • Longford • Roscommon
Castlerea • Boyle

Lakes dotted with small wooded islands are the main characteristic of County Roscommon. Beautifully situated on the north bank of the River Boyle at the foot of the Curlew Hills, the town of Boyle offers excellent river and lake fishing, golf and tennis. Close to the river at the north end of town are impressive ruins of the *Cistercian abbey*, founded in the 12th century. Most of the monks had come from Mellifont, the first Cistercian foundation in Ireland, and its French designs are strongly evident in the earliest, eastern part of the church at Boyle. The chancel is barrel-vaulted and each transept has two chapels. The abbey was used as a barracks in the 17th century by Cromwell's troops, when much damage was done to some of the main buildings, although the kitchen and hospital are still well preserved. The original splendour of this hallowed place is re-created in the large-scale model of the monastery and its surrounds that can be seen in the first-floor gatehouse on the western side of the cloister, which has been well restored.

*In Ballymoe village, between Roscommon and Castlerea, you are guaranteed a warm and friendly welcome from people who continue a traditional way of life*

*Take the **N4** for 9 miles (14km) southeast to Carrick-on-Shannon.*

### Carrick-on-Shannon, Co Leitrim

**1** Chief town of Ireland's most sparsely populated county, Carrick-on-Shannon is also the smallest county town in the country, and was first given its charter by James I. The coming of the railway and the roads hit the town hard but the growing demand for pleasure boating gave it a reprieve. Its situation athwart the River Shannon and its links to the Shannon's navigational system makes this attractive town a major river-cruising centre. There is also good trout and coarse fishing in the Shannon and nearby lakes.

Among its best-preserved buildings are the 19th-century **Court House** and the **Protestant** church.

*Follow the **N4** southeast for 23 miles (37km) to Longford.*

### Longford, Co Longford

**2** Set on the south bank of the River Camlin, the market town of Longford traces back to 1400, when a Dominican priory was founded here. Nothing remains of that ancient establishment, but the slight ruins of a **castle** built in 1627 are incorporated into the old **military barracks**. In the town centre, the grey limestone, 19th-century **St Mel's Cathedral**, a classical building by J B Keane and a prominent landmark behind the church, is an interesting ecclesiastical museum, with religious

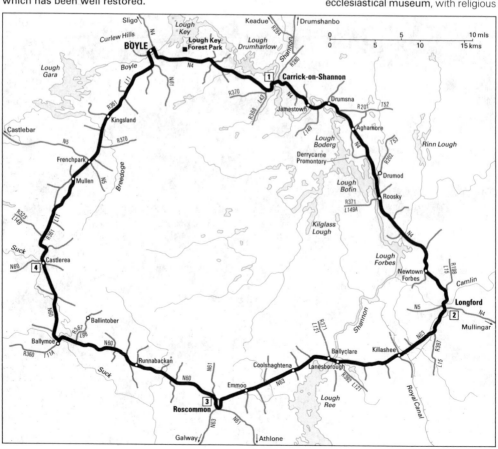

*The ruins of the Cistercian abbey at Boyle still show traces of its original splendour*

relics dating back prior to the penal years when there were restrictions on the Catholic religion.

Longford was a terminal of a branch of the Royal Canal, founded in 1789 and called the 'Shoemaker's Canal'.

*Take the N63 for 19 miles (31km) southwest to Roscommon.*

### Roscommon, Co Roscommon

**3** Situated at an important road junction, Roscommon is the county's chief town, named after St Coman, founder of an early 8th-century

Christian monastery here. Ruins of the **Dominican friary** are mainly 15th-century and include the 137-foot (42m) long, 23-foot (7m) wide church, with four pointed arches separating the aisle of the northern transept. A tomb in a burial niche in the north wall of the chancel is thought to be that of Felim O'Conor, King of Connacht, who founded the abbey in 1253. His effigy is perhaps the ruins' most interesting figure. The eight gallowglasses (mail-clad warriors) who support the tomb belonged originally to a much later tomb of about 1500.

*Boating is popular on Lough Key, one of Ireland's most beautiful lakes. The forest around it is rich in wildlife*

### RECOMMENDED WALK

**1** *Carrick-on-Shannon, Co Leitrim* At Carrick-on-Shannon, the walk from the town centre to the river bank and colourful marina is both interesting and scenic.

### SPECIAL TO ...

*Boyle, Co Roscommon* In August, the little town of **Keadue** (northeast of Boyle and Lough Key) rings with musical and sports events during the 10-day **O'Carolan Festival**, in memory of the last of the Irish bards, Turlough O'Carolan, who is buried in **Kilronan Church** cemetery, just northwest of the village.

**1** *Carrick-on-Shannon, Co Leitrim* **Drumshanbo**, 8 miles (13km) north of Carrick-on-Shannon on the **R280**, celebrates everything Irish – music, song, dance and pub events – in the **An Tostal Festival** each June.

### FOR HISTORY BUFFS

**3** *Roscommon, Co Roscommon* Ireland's last hangwoman, the legendary 'Lady Betty', is commemorated by a plaque on the 18th-century jail where she worked, and which was disused after 1822. Her own death sentence had been commuted when she agreed to take on the unwanted job of the hangman.

## BACK TO NATURE

*Boyle, Co Roscommon* **Lough Key Forest Park**, 2 miles (3km) east of Boyle on the **N4**, is one of Ireland's most beautiful scenic spots. The bog gardens are brilliant with rhododendron and azalea blooms in early summer, complemented by a wide variety of plants and shrubs that thrive in the peaty soil. The nature trail that winds through extensive forests is well marked with information on the many trees and plants along the way. **Moylurg Tower** tops a hill that once held a stately mansion, Rockingham House, (destroyed by fire), with fine views of the lake and woodlands.

## SCENIC ROUTES

Heading south from Carrick-on-Shannon on the **N4**, the road crosses a loop in the Shannon at Jamestown and again just before reaching **Drumsna**, a small town in an exceptionally scenic setting. As you continue southeast to Longford, the landscape is dotted with many small lakes that are part of the Shannon system. Two miles (3km) beyond **Aghamore**, an unclassified road to the right leads to the wooded Derrycarne promontory, which projects into Lough Boderg.

## FOR CHILDREN

*Boyle, Co Roscommon* Swimming, boating and other watersports are on offer at **Lough Key Forest Park**, 2 miles (3km) east of Boyle on the **N4**. Those who prefer to keep dry can enjoy the scenic lake cruises.

**4** *Castlerea, Co Roscommon* There are sports facilities and a swimming pool at Castlerea's **Demesne Park**.

*Bogland is a typical feature of the west of Ireland, and it supports a variety of plants*

Built in 1269 by Robert d'Ufford, the English Justiciar, but much altered since, **Roscommon Castle** was captured by the Irish four years later and razed to the ground. It was rebuilt in about 1280 and was besieged many times until the English Civil War, when it was held for the king by Sir Michael Earnley. It was surrendered to Cromwellian forces in 1652, who promptly dismantled it. The imposing ruins form a large quadrangular area, with a round bastion tower at each corner. The gateway is protected by two similar towers that project from the eastern wall. These appear to have been connected to the inner court, containing the state apartments.

*Take the **N60** northwest for 19 miles (31km) to Castlerea.*

### Castlerea, Co Roscommon

**4** This pretty little town was the birthplace, in 1815, of Oscar Wilde's father, Sir William Wilde, who was an antiquarian and oculist. Just west of town the fine 'great house' of Clonalis, rebuilt in the 19th century,

was the seat of the O'Conor Don, a direct descendant of the last High King of Ireland, who abdicated after the Anglo-Norman invasion of 1169. Ownership of such a manor house by a Gaelic family is unique, and Clonalis' furnishings reflect a more informal elegance than many other houses. The drawing room, for example, although beautifully furnished with Victoriana, is also a warm, comfortable room. Nineteenth-century portraits hang in the library, which also holds many fine books. There is a private chapel, and the highlight of the museum is the harp of Ireland's last great bard, Turlough O'Carolan (1670-1738), whose portrait is displayed. Among his compositions was the tune to which the *Star Spangled Banner* is now sung. Priceless Gaelic manuscripts, Victorian costumes, Sheraton furniture, porcelain and glass are also featured in the museum.

*Take the **R361 (L11)** for 17 miles (27km) north to Boyle.*

*A tranquil scene as the fishing boats come into Clew Bay at the end of the day. The bay is ringed with mountains and dotted with little islands*

# ACHILL ISLAND & COUNTY MAYO

Westport • Newport • Achill Island • Ballina • Knock
Tuam • Headford • Ballinrobe • Castlebar • Westport

---

ⓘ The Mall

*Take the **N59** north for 8 miles (13km) to Newport.*

## Newport, Co Mayo

**1** This picturesque little town, which dates from the 17th century, faces Clew Bay and is sheltered by mountains. It is a noted angling centre, with fishing on loughs Furnace, Beltra and Feeagh as well as in the rivers Burrishoole and Newport. Its neo-Romanesque Catholic **church** was built in 1914 and features a superb stained-glass window of the *Last Judgement* designed by Harry Clarke.

Four miles (6km) west of town, off the N59, **Rockfleet Castle**, sometimes called Carrigahowley Castle, is another of Grace O'Malley's strongholds. Dating from the 15th and 16th centuries, the tower dwelling has four storeys with a corner turret. The indomitable pirate queen came to live here permanently after her second husband died in 1583.

*Follow the **N59** west to Mulrany, then the **R319 (L141)** to Achill Island, 28 miles (45km).*

## Achill Island, Co Mayo

**2** The largest of Ireland's islands, Achill Island is connected to the mainland by a bridge. Only 15 miles (24km) long and 12 miles (19km) wide, its landscape is one of dramatic cliffs and seascapes, with a boggy, heather-covered interior. Fishing for shark and other big-game fish is

---

*Westport House, built in the Georgian style, was completed in the 1730s. It has a small formal garden*

---

**W**estport nestles in a hollow, and its lime-tree bordered Mall along each side of the Carrowbeg river is an attractive main artery. The town is notable for its splendid Georgian houses, traditional shopfronts, and the neo-Romanesque *St Mary's Catholic Church*. *Westport House*, a castle of the O'Malley clan, dates back to the 1730s. Designed by Richard Cassels and James Wyatt, it is filled with period furnishings, English and Irish art, silver, Waterford glass and chinaware. Visitors can go boating and fishing on the lake and river.

The most famous O'Malley was undoubtedly the 16th-century pirate queen, Grace. In Irish, she was known as 'Granuaile' and there is a fascinating *Granuaile Interpretive Centre* in Louisburg, some 12 miles (19km) west of Westport, via the *R335 (T39)*. The massive, square O'Malley *castle* overlooking the quay was modernised as a coastguard lookout in the 19th century and later used as a police barracks, but you can visit the *Carmelite friary* Grace's family founded in 1224, which has rare remains of fresco paintings. She is probably buried in the abbey graveyard.

## SCENIC ROUTES

**3** *Ballina, Co Mayo* An alternative route from Achill Island to Ballina takes you on a 48-mile (77km) loop around the north coast of County Mayo, through some of the finest cliff scenery in Ireland. Follow the **N59** north to Bangor Erris, then take the Belmullet road, the **R313 (T58)**, and just past Bunnahowen turn east on the **R314 (L133)** to Glenamoy, where an unclassified road turns left to reach the harbour of Portacloy. Returning to Glenamoy, proceed northeast on the **R314 (L133)** through Belderg and Ballycastle. Following the **R314 (L133)** south, you reach Killala, and 2 miles (3km) southeast of town, on a road to your left, is 15th-century Moyne Abbey. The **R314 (L133)** south takes you straight into Ballina.

## BACK TO NATURE

*Westport, Co Mayo* Ten miles (16km) west of Westport, 2 miles (3km) east of **Louisburg** and ½ mile (1km) on a signposted road off the **R335 (T39)**, the National Forest **Old Head Wood** provides a refreshing stop. There is a car park and also picnic grounds, with well-marked pathways through the small reserve. Oak is the dominant species, but shares the territory with native birch, willow and rowan. Beech and sycamore trees, not native to the area, have also been introduced. There are viewing points overlooking Clew Bay and its islands.

## RECOMMENDED WALKS

*Westport, Co Mayo* **Croagh Patrick**, 5 miles (8km) west of Westport via the **R335 (T39)**, rises some 2,510 feet (765m) above the shore of Clew Bay near the little town of Murrisk. This is Ireland's Holy Mountain, on which St Patrick is said to have spent the 40 days of Lent in 441, and where legend says he lured all the snakes in Ireland to the summit, then rang his bell as a signal for all to throw themselves over a precipice. It is an easy climb that takes only about an hour by way of a path from Murrisk.

excellent, with boats and guides for hire. There are also very good bathing beaches, and the beautiful **Atlantic Drive** around the island climbs from gently rolling mountain foothills, past stretches of sandy beaches, and through tiny picturesque villages with excellent views of the sea, Clew Bay and the mainland. At **Kildownet**, another Grace O'Malley **castle** is well preserved, and ruins of a small 12th-century **church** are nearby.

At the centre of holiday activities is **Keel**, which has a fine sandy beach and a small harbour with fishing or sightseeing boats for hire. Indeed, seen from a boat, the sea-carved rocks below the Menawn cliffs at the eastern end of the beach take on fanciful shapes.

At **Doogort**, nestled at the foot of Slievemore, boatmen take visitors to the fascinating **Seal Caves** cut far into the cliffs of Slievemore.

*Take the* **R319 (L141)** *back to Mulrany, then turn north on the* **N59** *for the 47-mile (76km) drive to Ballina, passing through Ballycroy and Bangor Erris (where the* **N59** *turns sharply east).*

---

*Ballina is the largest town in County Mayo. It is on the River Moy and is a famous centre for salmon and trout fishing*

## Ballina, Co Mayo

**3** An important angling centre on the River Moy and near Lough Conn, Ballina is County Mayo's largest town. Founded in 1730, it is also a cathedral town, and near its 19th-century **Cathedral of St Muiredach**, which has a fine stained glass window, are ruins of a 15th-century **Augustinian friary**. About 3 miles (5km) north of Ballina, the 15th-century **Rosserk Friary** sits peacefully on the shore of Killala Bay. The ruins include a tower, a small cloister, nave, chancel, a fine arched doorway and east window.

Eight miles (13km) north of Ballina via the **R314**, **Killala**, the small harbour where General Humbert and his French forces landed in 1798, has a wealth of antiquities in the immediate vicinity, as well as one of the finest round towers in the country. Nearby Franciscan **Moyne Abbey** was founded in the mid-15th century. Although burned in 1590, the well-preserved ruins include a six-storey square tower, vaulted chapter room, and a partially vaulted sacristy.

*Take the* **N57** *south then southeast for 18 miles (29km), through Foxford to Swinford. Follow the* **R320 (L27)** *for 7 miles (11km) south to Kiltimagh, then turn southeast on the* **R323 (L140)** *for 5 miles (8km) to reach Knock.*

### Knock, Co Mayo

**4** This small town was the setting of an apparition in 1879, the central figure of which was the Blessed Virgin. After intensive investigation by Catholic authorities, it was declared authentic and named a Marian shrine. A large, circular **church** has been built to accommodate the huge pilgrimages to the town, with 32 pillars in the ambulatory contributed by all counties in the country, and four windows in medieval style that represent the four provinces of Ireland. Its finest hour came in 1979 when Pope John Paul II came on an official visit.

The **Knock Folk Museum** exhibits relics of rural and small-town life in this part of Ireland.

*Take the **N17** south for 25 miles (40km) to Tuam.*

### Tuam, Co Galway

**5** A thriving commercial and agricultural centre under James I's charter of 1613, the layout of Tuam was altered to include a diamond-shaped town 'square' on which all roads converged. The 19th-century Church of Ireland **St Mary's Cathedral**, founded in 1130 and rebuilt largely in the 19th century, is a fine example of Gothic-revival architecture and incorporates a 12th-century chancel with magnificent windows. A slightly earlier Roman Catholic **Cathedral of**

**the Assumption** is a marvellous neo-Gothic building with fine window and tower carvings. In the town square, the **high cross** of Tuam, dating from the 12th century, is well adorned but incomplete. Tuam can claim Ireland's first industrial museum, the **Mill Museum**, an operational corn mill with mill-wheel and interesting industrial exhibits.

About 1½ miles (2.5km) east of town on the Ryehill road, there is an interesting medieval lake dwelling known as **Loughpark Crannóg**. Seven miles (11km) to the southeast on the shores of a small lake is the 12th-century **Knockmoy Abbey**. The tomb of its founder, Cathal O'Connor, King of Connacht, can be found in the ruins, as can traces of ancient murals on the north wall of the chancel.

*Leave Tuam on the **N17** southwest, and about 3 miles (5km) from town turn west on the **R333 (L98)** for 9 miles (14km) to reach Headford.*

### Headford, Co Galway

**6** This popular angling and market centre is very close to Lough Corrib, and there are boats for hire at nearby **Greenfield**. Two miles (3km) northwest of town, **Ross Abbey** is a large 1498 Franciscan friary that fell victim to Cromwellian forces in 1656. Its original size can be judged by its two

Good! TOUR!

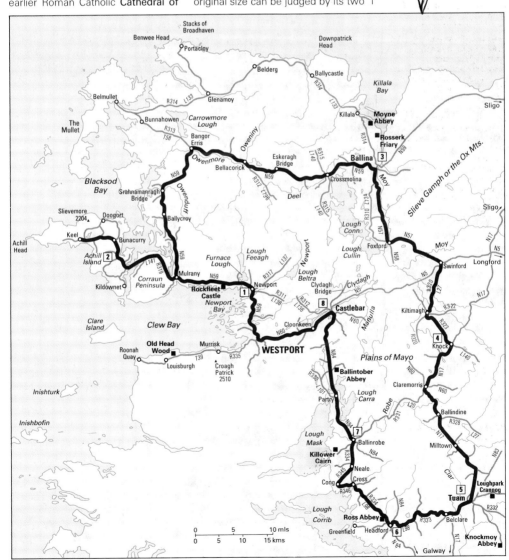

7 *Ballinrobe, Co Mayo* About 10 miles (16km) north of Ballinrobe, just beyond Partry on the **N84**, **Ballintober Abbey** is unique in the English-speaking world in that mass has been celebrated continuously since its foundation in 1216. It was suppressed by Henry VIII in 1542, the roof was removed by Cromwellians in 1653 and the central tower collapsed. The Penal Laws in the 18th century applied here as well as elsewhere in Ireland. Despite all this, celebrants continued to come to whatever was left of the abbey. Renovation was completed in time for the 750th anniversary ceremonies in 1966.

---

*Westport, Co Mayo*
Westport's **Street Festival** in July features street performers and folk singers from all over Ireland, who come here to perform.

8 *Castlebar, Co Mayo*
Castlebar's **International Walking Festival** is a highlight of each June.

*Impressive Ashford Castle, near Cong, was built in a variety of styles, and at one time belonged to the Guinness family. It is now a luxury hotel*

---

courtyards, around which are the domestic buildings. These include a refectory with reader's desk, dormitories, and a kitchen with a surprising forerunner of modern fish tanks.

> *Take the **R334 (L98)** northwest for just over 6 miles (10km), then turn left to Cong via the **R346 (L98A)**. From Cong take the **R345 (L101)** northeast to rejoin the **R334 (L98)** and turn left to reach Ballinrobe.*

**Ballinrobe, Co Mayo**

7 Beautifully situated in the vicinity of three good fishing lakes (loughs Corrib, Mask and Carra), this small town is surrounded by mountains and woodlands. At the north end of town are the ruins of a 1313 **Augustinian** friary, and about 3 miles (5km) to the southwest is **Killower Cairn**, one of the most impressive in Connacht.

Just 7 miles (11km) south of Ballinrobe (take the **R334** and turn west on the **R345**), the little town of Cong was the setting for most of the popular film, *The Quiet Man*. That, however, is the least of its claims to fame. More notable are the ruins of the **Royal Abbey of Cong**, built by Turlough Mor O'Connor, High King of Ireland in the 12th century on the site of a 7th-century monastic community,

and burial place of Ireland's last High King, Rory O'Connor, who died in 1198; the impressive **Ashford Castle**, now a luxury hotel, whose rather eccentric architecture incorporates several styles and periods; and the 14th-century inscribed **stone cross** in the main street.

> *Follow the **N84** for 18 miles (29km) north to Castlebar.*

**Castlebar, Co Mayo**

8 The county town of Mayo, Castlebar has figured in several major Irish insurrections, most notably in 1798, when Irish-French forces routed British cavalry, causing such a hasty retreat to Hollymount, Tuam and Athlone that the campaign gained the nickname 'The Race of Castlebar'. The present **Imperial Hotel** was known as James Daly's Hotel in 1879 when the Land League was founded there.

About 2 miles (3km) northeast from town **Clydagh Bridge** is the starting point for an idyllic forest walk.

> *Take the **N60** southwest for the 11-mile (18km) drive back to Westport.*

---

Westport – Newport **8 (13)**
Newport – Achill Island **28 (45)**
Achill Island – Ballina **56 (90)**
Ballina – Knock **30 (48)**
Knock – Tuam **25 (40)**
Tuam – Headford **12 (19)**
Headford – Ballinrobe **19 (31)**
Ballinrobe – Castlebar **18 (29)**
Castlebar – Westport **11 (18)**

*Connemara's Sky Drive skirts the peninsula and gives good views across Clifden Bay. It also provides glimpses of the west's traditional way of life*

ℹ️ Aras Failte, Victoria Place

*Take the coast road, the **R336** (**L100**), west for 11 miles (18km) to Spiddal.*

## Spiddal, Co Galway

**1** This charming little resort town has a marvellous beach, the **Silver Strand**, and shore fishing is especially good here. Its Roman Catholic **St Eanna's Church** is an architectural delight, completed in 1904 in Celtic Romanesque style by William A Scott.

A favourite pastime during the summer are races between local curraghs (lightweight wood and canvas boats). Look for the **Spiddal Craft Centre**, a complex of craft workshops and showrooms.

*Continue west on the **R336** (**L100**) for 12 miles (19km) to Rossaveel, which lies just off this road.*

## Rossaveel, Co Galway

**2** There are still thatched cottages scattered about this small harbour, from which turf is shipped by barge to the Aran Islands. The passenger boat trip out to the islands is only 1 hour from Rossaveel as compared to the 2½-hour voyage from Galway.

The **Aran Islands** group consists of three inhabited islands: Inishmore, with the only safe harbour for steamers; Inishmaan and Inisheer, where curraghs meet incoming boats to take passengers or freight to the docks.

*Ruined cottages at Roundstone with Errisbeg (987 feet/300m) in the background*

# REGION OF STONY BEAUTY

Galway • Spiddal • Rossaveel • Screeb • Gortmore
Carna • Roundstone • Clifden • Kylemore Abbey • Leenane
Maam Cross • Oughterard • Galway

**A** thriving commercial centre, Galway takes pride in its university and active cultural life. The *Bank of Ireland*, on Eyre (pronounced 'Air') Square, displays the 17th-century civic sword and great mace, both splendid examples of Irish silverwork. Just down the square, *Spanish Arch* is one of the gateways in the old city walls. The adjacent small *City Museum* houses interesting artefacts, and its spiral staircase leads to a gallery that in turn leads to an open terrace with good views of the harbour and city.

At the corner of Abbeygate and Shop streets, look for *Lynch's Castle*, a superb medieval town house that now houses the Allied Irish Bank. *St Nicholas' Collegiate Church*, off Shop Street, dates back to 1320. Its proudest claim is that Christopher Columbus stopped here for mass in 1492.

Galway has two noteworthy theatres; *Taibhdhearc Theatre* (Thive-yark') in Middle Street, and the *Druid Theatre* in Chapel Lane. Nearby *Dunguaire Castle* has an excellent medieval banquet and literary evening during summer months.

## FOR HISTORY BUFFS

*Galway, Co Galway* Take a look at the **Lynch Memorial Window** in Market Street. There is an inscription above the Gothic doorway. The story goes that Lord Mayor James Lynch FitzStephen's popular 19-year-old son murdered one of his closest friends, who he thought paid undue attention to a young lady they both admired. Overcome with remorse, the son turned himself in, and his father sat as magistrate in the case, returning a death-by-hanging sentence. When the executioner refused to perform his duty, the father carried out the sentence himself.

## RECOMMENDED WALKS

**6** *Roundstone, Co Galway* About 2 miles (3km) from Roundstone on the Ballyconneely road (**R341**), leave the car at Dog's Bay and walk its beautiful sandy beach around the coast to **Gorteen Bay**, which also has a lovely sandy beach. **Errisbeg Mountain**, which hovers over this part of Connemara, is an easy climb, with magnificent views of the lakes and stony landscape to the north and fine seascapes that reach as far as Clifden to the northwest and the **Twelve Pins** to the northeast.

Prehistory has left its mark on the faces of all three – promontory forts, ringforts and beehive huts speak of the 'Celtic Twilight' era, while round towers, oratories and tiny churches are reminders of the early days of Christianity in Ireland.

A visit to the Arans is an easy, delightful day-trip from Rossaveel, and accommodation can be arranged in advance for those who want to stay longer. Steamers to **Inishmore**, the largest of the islands, dock at the main port of Kilronan, and jaunting cars are waiting to take visitors exploring. Rented bicycles are also available, and walkers will delight in following the one main road around the island, with an occasional stop to chat with its local inhabitants.

**Dun Aengus** is an 11-acre (4.5-hectare) stone fort perched on a cliff some 300 feet (91m) above the sea, one of the finest prehistoric monuments in western Europe. Its three concentric enclosures are surrounded by dry stone walls, and the innermost rampart is just the place for outstanding views of the islands and the Connemara coast.

Near the village of **Cowrugh**, the grounds of a small 15th-century church hold four great flagstones marking the graves of saints, and south of the church there is a holy well. The area surrounding this village is littered with ancient monuments. But, then, it is literally impossible to go very far on this large island or the two smaller ones without encountering a vivid reminder of centuries past in one form or another.

Among the remains on **Inisheer** are the medieval tower of **O'Brien's Castle** which is situated on a prominent rocky hill, **St Gobnet's Church** and the **Church of St Cavan**.

The oval fort of **Dun Conor** rises

from a steep-sided hill on **Inishmaan**; there is also a fine dolmen.

Visits to Inishmaan and Inisheer can be arranged with boatmen in Kilronan.

*Turn north on the* **R336 (L100)** *for 9 miles (14km) to Screeb.*

### Screeb, Co Galway

**3** There is excellent game fishing from this small town. Also, one of Ireland's peat-burning electricity generating stations is in the near vicinity.

*Turn west on to the* **R340 (L102)** *for the 3-mile (5km) drive to Gortmore.*

### Gortmore, Co Galway

**4** From this village, a turn left will take you to the town of Tuar Loch, site of **Padraig Pearse's cottage**. It was in this small thatched cottage that the great Irish leader, who was executed in 1916, spent his holidays and wrote his most important works.

*Follow the* **R340 (L102)** *southwest for 12 miles (19km) to Carna.*

### Carna, Co Galway

**5** Lobster fishing is still the main occupation in this picturesque village. Three miles (5km) to the south, a bridge connects Miveenish Island to the mainland. The beautiful beaches and interesting University College Galway **marine biology station** make a worthwhile detour.

You can take a boat to **St Macdara's Island**, named after the 6th-century saint who lived here with other hermits.

*Take the* **R340 (L102)** *north for about 7 miles (11km), then turn west on to the* **R342** *(signposted*

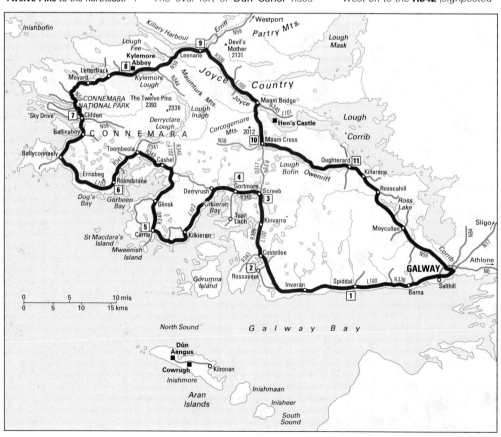

*Cashel) for 5 miles (8km) and at Toombeola turn south on to the **R341 (L102)** for the 4-mile (6km) drive to Roundstone.*

## Roundstone, Co Galway

**6** This pretty village on the west side of Roundstone Bay is a relaxing, quiet holiday resort that in recent years has attracted a host of artists and craftspeople as permanent residents. Look for their workshops and showrooms. The settlement here was originally established in the early 19th century for Scottish fishermen.

About 2 miles (3km) out on the Ballyconneely road is a fine sandy beach at **Dog's Bay** (Port-na-Feadog).

*Continue on the **R341 (L102)** northwest for 13 miles (21km) to Clifden.*

---

*The Twelve Pins seen from near Roundstone. Conical in shape, they are a dominant feature of the Connemara landscape and occupy an area 6 miles (9.5km) in diameter*

**FOR CHILDREN**

*Galway, Co Galway* West of Galway, **Salthill** is a children's paradise. In addition to a good beach and pedal buggies for riding along the promenade, attractions at **Leisureland Amusement Park** are guaranteed to please. The huge complex includes a heated indoor pool, a superb waterslide and just about every ride known to humankind.

### Clifden, Co Galway

**7** Nestled between the mountains and the Atlantic, with the **Twelve Pins** (or Bens) rising to its east, Clifden is often called 'The Capital of Connemara'. It lies at the head of Clifden Bay. Built in the 19th century, the town has managed to keep its Georgian character. Its two churches dominate the skyline, and the 1830 **Catholic church** is built on the site of an ancient beehive monastic stone hut, a *clochan*, which gave the town its name. The 1820 **Protestant church** is also a fine structure and holds a silver copy of the **Cross of Cong**. **Clifden Castle** was built by John D'Arcy in 1815. Its grounds give a fine marine view.

Clifden is the very centre of Connemara pony breeding country, and you are in luck if you arrive in August during the annual **Connemara Pony Show**. The sturdy little Connemara ponies are native to the area, and are much in demand. It is great fun to see the trading, and the festivities also include exhibitions of Irish arts and crafts.

About 4 miles (6km) south of Clifden (1½ miles, (2.5km) north of Ballyconneely), look for signposts to the **Alcock and Brown Memorial**, the spot in **Derrygimlagh Bog** where these intrepid aviators crash-landed at the end of the first non-stop flight across the Atlantic from St John's, Newfoundland, in 1919. About 1½ miles (2.5km) away stands a limestone aeroplane erected in their honour.

*Clifden is in the heart of Connemara. Its skyline is dominated by two churches, and the Twelve Pins can be seen in the distance*

Near by are masts and foundations of the first transatlantic wireless transmitting station, set up here by Marconi, the Italian pioneer of radio.

*Take the **N59** northeast for 11 miles (18km) to Kylemore Abbey.*

### Kylemore Abbey, Co Galway

**8** Situated in the scenic Pass of Kylemore, palatial Kylemore Abbey looks less like an ecclesiastical institution than any other in Ireland. Not surprising, since this magnificent gleaming white castellated mansion was built in the late 1800s as a private residence for millionaire MP Mitchell Henry. Its setting is enhanced by the castle's shimmering image reflected in the waters of one of the three Kylemore lakes. Now a convent of the Benedictine Nuns of Ypres, it also houses a pottery and a restaurant run by the nuns. Visitors are welcomed to both, as well as to the lovely grounds and the Gothic chapel.

En route to Leenane, the Maamturk mountain range comes into view, with loughs Fee and Nacarrigeen on your left. Further on, the road follows the southern shore of **Killary harbour**, a 10-mile (16km) long fiord-like inlet from the sea that runs between steep mountains.

*Continue northeast on the **N59** for 9 miles (14km) to Leenane.*

## Leenane, Co Galway

**9** Set near the head of Killary harbour, Leenane is a popular angling centre and mountain-climbing base. This is the western end of the **Partry Mountains**, and the 2,131-foot (650m) **Devil's Mother** is the most striking feature of the landscape around this lovely village. Close to Leenane (on the road to Louisburgh) is the beautiful **Aasleagh waterfall**, which is well worth a short detour.

*Turn southeast on to the **R336** (**L100**) for 13 miles (21km) to Maam Cross.*

## Maam Cross, Co Galway

**10** This crossroads between north and south Connemara runs through some of the region's most beautiful scenery. Local mountain peaks are relatively easy to climb and provide marvellous views. For good views of **Lough Corrib** and its fabled **Castlekirk** (the Hen's Castle), a 13th-century keep built by Rory O'Connor, take the road north signposted Maam and turn right at the T-junction. According to legend, Castlekirk was built overnight by a witch and her hen.

*Squeezed between lake and hillside, Kylemore Abbey was built as a private residence, and is now a convent*

*Continue southeast on the **N59** for 10 miles (16km) to Oughterard.*

## Oughterard, Co Galway

**11** This lively town on the upper shores of Lough Corrib is also a popular salmon and trout angling resort. Views along the loughside road are especially impressive, and local boatmen take visitors on excursions to the many islands. You can see beautiful Hill of Don by following the loughside road north. **Aughnanure Castle**, built by the O'Flaherty's in about 1500, is a six-storey tower house lying in an idyllic setting near the shores of Lough Corrib.

**Ross Lake** and **Ross Castle** lie 5 miles (8km) southeast of Oughterard. Here Violet Martin collaborated with her cousin Edith Somerville on *Experiences of an Irish RM* and other novels.

*Follow the **N59** southeast for 17 miles (27km) to Galway.*

Galway – Spiddal **11 (18)**
Spiddal – Rossaveel **12 (19)**
Rossaveel – Screeb **9 (14)**
Screeb – Gortmore **3 (5)**
Gortmore – Carna **12 (19)**
Carna – Roundstone **16 (26)**
Roundstone – Clifden **13 (21)**
Clifden – Kylemore Abbey **11 (18)**
Kylemore Abbey – Leenane **9 (14)**
Leenane – Maam Cross **13 (21)**
Maam Cross – Oughterard **10 (16)**
Oughterard – Galway **17 (27)**

---

### BACK TO NATURE

**8** *Kylemore Abbey, Co Galway* Between Kylemore Abbey and Letterfrack, the **Connemara National Park** covers some 4,940 acres (2,000 hectares) that encompass virtually all varieties of this unique region's geology, flora and fauna. Four peaks of the Twelve Pins mountain range are here, surrounded by boglands, heaths and grasslands. Western blanket bog and heathland are the most common vegetation. The bogs are dotted with clumps of purple moor-grass, bog asphodel, bog myrtle and bog cotton. Insect-eating sundews and butterworts, milkwort, orchids and a variety of lichens and mosses also grow here. Birds of prey such as sparrowhawks, merlins, peregrines and kestrels are seen from time to time. Red deer, once native to the hills of Connemara, are being reintroduced, and there is a well established herd of Connemara ponies. Detailed literature on the park is available at the Visitor Centre.

# ULSTER

IRELAND

Ulster is a beautiful place, rich in history, rare in scenery, a province of mountains, loughs, coast and countryside, with tranquil villages and friendly people. The ancient province of Ulster had nine counties: Antrim, Down, Londonderry, Fermanagh, Tyrone and Armagh, which now form Northern Ireland; and Donegal, Cavan and Monaghan, which are part of the Republic of Ireland.

When Patrick came to Celtic Ireland, he chose Armagh for his ecclesiastical capital, because of the strength of Emain Macha, the Palace of the Red Branch Knights. Ulster made a contribution to Ireland's claim to be a land of saints and scholars. Great monasteries and educational establishments were founded, like that at Bangor, in County Down, which sent out missionaries to light up the Dark Age of Europe.

Since Patrick's time the province, like the rest of Ireland, has had successive waves of invaders. Vikings, Normans, English, Scots, Huguenots and refugees have settled here. However, in Ulster it was the number of Scots and Celts, but mostly Presbyterians, that created the special blend of Planter and Gael in Ulster. The hardy race of Scots-Ulster had a temperament tough enough to cope with the frontiers of the New World of America, and enterprising enough to leave a land where non-Conformists were at a disadvantage. A dozen American presidents came from this stock. These were the men who defended Derry in the siege, fought with William at the Boyne, won glory for their bravery at the Somme and refused to join a united Ireland in the 1920s.

There is evidence of the two distinctive traditions in Ulster – fife and drum, uillean pipes and bodhran, paintings of King Billy or Mother Ireland on gable walls (most likely drawn by the same man). However, you may be surprised at how little difference there is between the two.

Ulster has a tradition of good food and local specialities include excellent seafood, salmon and trout, fresh game in season, County Antrim turkey and ham, and dulse, a type of edible seaweed.

Ulster people are delighted to see visitors and very anxious to show them the best of their province. Local councils have worked hard to provide fine amenities in even the most out-of-the-way places. Small villages are festooned with hanging baskets, window boxes and flower-filled carts give the best impression. When Ulster people are really enjoying themselves – and they do, often – they say 'It's great crack'. 'Crack' is fun, music, laughter and story-telling, often washed down with a drink or two, and they will be happy to share 'the crack' with visitors.

## Tour 20

From historic walled Derry, a proud city rich in song and humour, the tour enters Donegal, whose incomparable scenery is world-renowned – empty beaches stretching for miles are commonplace, amid a landscape of rugged hills, stone walls and white cottages crouching against the Atlantic. The tour passes through fishing and farming communities where the Irish language and traditions are cherished, and ends with Donegal's treasure, Glenveagh National Park.

## Tour 21

The Antrim Coast road, which clings to the shore between glens and mountains, headlands and villages, begins a drive of stunning variety. The Giant's Causeway is an essential destination for every traveller to this part of Ireland, but the tour takes in lesser known delights, as well as dramatic castles and historic landscapes, returning to the port of Larne through the pleasant countryside of north Antrim.

## Tour 22

Belfast, a city of character, is the starting point for a tour that is full of interest for those who love history and wildlife or who simply enjoy discovering quiet villages in beautiful settings. The route takes in the Ulster Folk Museum, the two fine country houses of Mount Stewart and Castle Ward, and important early Christian sites. The tour focuses on Strangford Lough. The steep sides of the land around the narrows of the lough, where fast running tides have helped to create a habitat rich in marine biology, in an area no less important to ornithologists.

## Tour 23

Fermanagh is a very distinctive Ulster county, more water than land it seems, and the land is sparsely populated. The combination of water, woodland and ancient buildings is nowhere so varied as in Fermanagh. The tranquil waters of Lough Erne offer a fisherman's paradise. The route begins in the historic town of Enniskillen and includes the haunting beauty of the monastic round tower at Devenish and the neoclassical splendour of Castle Coole. Belleek pottery and Marble Arch caves provide additional interest.

## Tour 24

Armagh, the ecclesiastical capital of Ireland, is the starting point for a tour that climbs from the gentle pastures and orchards of County Armagh to the rugged mountains of County Tyrone. This is a journey through Ulster's history, from the heroic era of the Red Branch Knights and the coming of Saint Patrick to the Irish emigrants' new world of America. Country houses, glens and forests, peatlands and parkland come together to form a picture of mid-Ulster.

## Tour 25

County Down's distinctive landscape is that of the drumlins, small rounded hills that roll and roll, sheltering quiet

green valleys and offering sudden views of sea or lough. The route leaves Newry and goes by way of the charming village of Hillsborough, and then winds through hills again until they give way to the Mountains of Mourne. The Kingdom of Mourne has its own identity, from the small fishing harbours of the rocky coast, through farmland crisscrossed by stone walls to the heights of the

*Top: A quiet, tranquil scene on Glenveagh Lough.*
*Above: One of the old cottages used for storing peat at Dunlewy, in the Poisoned Glen*

mountains. The end of the journey takes in beautiful Carlingford Lough, abundant in forests, castles and pleasant resorts.

# SEASCAPES & MOUNTAIN PASSES

Londonderry • Grianan of Aileach • Letterkenny • Rathmelton
Rathmullan • Milford • Carrigart • The Atlantic Drive
Creeslough • Dunfanaghy • Errigal Mountain
Glenveagh • Londonderry

*The ruins of the marble church near the hamlet of Dunlewy, on the south side of Mount Errigal. At 2,466 feet (752m), Errigal is the highest mountain in Donegal and provides extensive views*

ℹ️ Foyle Street

*Take the A2 for Buncrana, then the N13 to Letterkenny to the sign for Grianan of Aileach.*

## The Grianan of Aileach, Co Donegal

**1** This massive **stone fort** can be seen for miles around, and the climb to Grianan Mountain gives majestic views over Lough Foyle and Lough Swilly. It is easy to see why this commanding site should have been chosen for the royal residence of the O'Neills, Kings of Ulster. It was enthusiastically restored by Dr Bernard of Derry in 1870, and his work has left us with a complete picture of walls 17 feet (5.25m) high and 13 feet (4m) thick, with steps rising to four levels. The fine modern **church** at **Burt** has architectural echoes of Grianan.

*Return to the N13 and turn left to follow it for 18 miles (29km) to Letterkenny.*

## Letterkenny, Co Donegal

**2** An administrative and commercial centre in the northwest, Letterkenny sits at the southwest end of Lough Swilly on a fertile plain. In the 19th century it was spoken of as 'fast becoming a place of importance and wealth' and had a steamer communication with Glasgow. It gained the richly Gothic **St Eunan's Cathedral** at the end of the last century.

ℹ️ Derry Road

*Take the R245 (T72) for 8 miles (13km) to Rathmelton.*

## Rathmelton, Co Donegal

**3** The long curve of the River Leannan, steep hills, tree-lined streets and handsome warehouses on the riverfront all combine to make Rathmelton a place of great charm. It

**Y**ou will be instantly aware of the history around you in Londonderry, popularly known as Derry, from the network of walls, gates and bastions, the most complete in the British Isles, and their cannons, the most famous of which is *'Roaring Meg'*. Derry, 'the Maiden City', was impregnable even in 1689, when the city held out desperately against James II's forces in the Williamite wars. Look out for *Coward's Bastion*, which was furthest from the heavy fighting, and *Hangman's Bastion*, where a man trying to escape by being lowered on a rope was almost throttled.

The fine *Guildhall* has been rebuilt several times and dominates the riverside, while *St Eugene's Cathedral's* spire soars above. *St Columb's Cathedral* was built in the 17th century. Today, Derry enjoys a flourishing arts scene, and also offers a craft village, and a developing historic focus in *O'Doherty's Tower*.

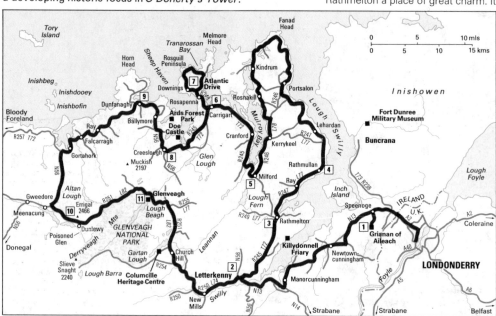

was a Planters' town ('planters' were Presbyterian Scots and Anglican English settlers loyal to the English crown who were encouraged to settle in Ireland and replace the rebellious Catholic Irish landowners). Prosperity gained by the easy navigation from the river mouth brought fine Georgian houses, as well as corn mills, a brewery, bleach greens and linen works in the early 19th century. The first Presbyterian church in America was organised in 1706 by Reverend Francis Makemie, an emigrant from Rathmelton. Anglers come here to fish, and 'The Pool', nearby, is a well-known salmon beat.

**Killydonnell Friary**, founded by the Franciscans in the 16th century, is 2½ miles (4km) to the south in the grounds of **Fort Stewart**. There are excellent views of the surrounding countryside from **Cam Hill**.

*Take the **R247 (L77)** for 7 miles (11km) to Rathmullan.*

### Rathmullan, Co Donegal

**4** Rathmullan is a pretty village fringed with trees, on a beautiful beach on Lough Swilly, looking over to the hills of the Inishowen peninsula, with the ruin of a 16th-century **priory** at the water's edge. Quite large fishing ships come into its pier, without upsetting the tranquillity. Despite its present peacefulness, Rathmullan has witnessed two major historical events. In 1587, Red Hugh O'Donnell was treacherously lured on board a disguised merchant ship and carried as prisoner to Dublin Castle, and that evocative moment in Irish history, the Flight of the Earls, took place from here in 1607. The O'Neill, Earl of Tyrone and the O'Donnell, Earl of Tyrconnell, with about a hundred lesser chieftains, finally gave up their resistance to English law and authority in Ulster, and left for exile in Europe, leaving their estates to be forfeited and colonised by English and Scottish settlers. A **Heritage Centre** in Rathmullan tells the story.

Rathmullan is at the start of the **Fanad Drive**, with its beaches, streams, lakes and mountain ridges.

*Follow the signposts for the Fanad Drive by Portsalon and Kerrykeel to Milford, 31 miles (50km).*

*The sun sets over the delightful and remote Tranarossan Bay, at the northern end of the Rosguill Peninsula, a rocky headland with sandy beaches, good fishing and wonderful views of the coastline*

### Milford, Co Donegal

**5** Milford offers a contrast to the grand headlands and magnificent bays of Donegal. It stands at the end of the narrow, islanded inlet of Mulroy Bay, and among its wooded hills are two lovely glens with the waterfalls **Golan Loop** and **Grey Mare's Tail**.

*Take the **R245 (T72)** for 10 miles (16km) to Carrigart.*

### Carrigart, Co Donegal

**6** This busy little town is tucked in an inlet of Mulroy Bay. To the north is **Rosapenna**, which boasts a championship golf course that is as scenic as it is challenging.

Nature challenged man and won in the 18th century, when a massive sandstorm engulfed houses and gradually overtook Rosapenna House, finally forcing the occupant, the Reverend Porter, from the top floor in 1808. From Rosapenna beach you can see the **Muslac caves**, cut by the sea into quartzite folds. **The Downings** is a small resort, particularly popular with families with small children, and has an important tweed factory and shop.

*Follow the signs for the Atlantic Drive.*

### The Atlantic Drive, Co Donegal

**7** It is held that the feast of scenery along the road around the Rosguill Peninsula, called the Atlantic Drive, is Donegal's best. The spectacular circuit passes both **Sheep Haven** and **Mulroy** bays, **Horn Head** and **Melmore Head** are in focus, with **Muckish** and **Errigal** mountains more distant to the south. The road passes little shingly bays, and hillsides dotted with white cottages, then opens out to the incomparable sight of **Tranarossan Strand**. Here the Youth Hostel is in an idiosyncratic building designed by the architect, Lutyens.

*Return to Carrigart and follow the **R245 (T72)** for 7 miles (11km) to Creeslough.*

### RECOMMENDED WALKS

**2** **Letterkenny, Co Donegal**
Pick any deserted beach for a bracing walk, take a town trail in Letterkenny, or try one of the forest and woodland paths.

**8** **Creeslough, Co Donegal**
At **Ards Forest Park**, near Creeslough, Lough Lilly is rich with flowering water-lilies in high summer and an enclosed park contains deer. At this most northerly forest park, the trees go right down to the sea, and there are places to bathe, as well as walk.

### SCENIC ROUTES

In this rugged part of Donegal it would be easier to mention those roads that are not scenic. Try the circuit around **Bloody Foreland** with its sheltered beaches, small fishing inlets, stone-walled fields and white cottages. Look for islands – **Gola** to the west, **Inishbofin**, **Inishdooey**, **Inishbeg** and **Tory** to the north, and learn that Bloody Foreland, the northwest tip of Ireland, gets its name, not from a grisly past, but from the red granite boulders that glow in the setting sun.

**9** *Dunfanaghy, Co Donegal*
**Marble Hill**, 4 miles (6km)
to the east of Dunfanaghy, is
a safe and beautiful strand,
where windsurfing and
canoeing have been tailored
for children, with special
lessons, and the right size of
wetsuits and equipment.
Over 10-year-olds, even those
with no experience, can join a
canoe expedition. Basic
instruction is given, and the
expeditions, under qualified
supervision, offer an ideal
introduction to the joys of
canoeing in magnificent
surroundings.

### Creeslough, Co Donegal

**8** On a height overlooking Sheep
Haven Bay is the little village of
Creeslough. **Doe Castle** stands on a
low, narrow promontory, bounded by
the sea on three sides and a rock-cut
ditch on the fourth. It is fortified with
corbelled bartizans or turrets, firing
platforms and musket loops, a round
tower and a great square keep. It has
had a colourful and turbulent history.
It became the stronghold of the
MacSweeneys, who were 'gallowglasses' (foreign warriors), a
professional fighting force invited by
the O'Donnell from Scotland. It was a
refuge for Spanish Armada sailors,
was taken by the Cromwellians and
was used as a garrison for William of
Orange. Finally it came into the hands
of an English family, the Harts. The
initials of General George Vaughan
Hart are over the door.

> *Follow the signs for Dunglow,
> then take the **N56** for 7 miles
> (11km) to Dunfanaghy.*

### Dunfanaghy, Co Donegal

**9** This is a neat, bustling little place,
a good point from which to explore
Horn Head, thought by many to be the
finest of all Irish headlands – a wall of
quartzite rising from the sea, the
ledges alive with gulls, puffins,
guillemots and razorbills. You can
appreciate the full majesty of Horn
from Traghlisk Point to the east.

To the northwest is **Tory Island**, still
inhabited by people who make their
living from the sea. The art world has
considerable respect for the naïve
paintings of the Tory Island artists. To
the southwest is **Falcarragh**, the best
point from which to climb the flat-
topped mountain, Muckish.

[i] McAuliffe's Shop

> *Continue on the **N56** for 7 miles
> (11km) to Falcarragh, then 2½
> miles (4km) to Gortahork. Take a
> left fork for Dunglow on the **N56**.*

*The resort of Gortahork, near
Ballyness Bay*

SPECIAL TO...

**9** *Dunfanaghy, Co Donegal*
Irish is the first language of many people in Donegal. The **Gaeltacht** is the name given to the areas where the language is widely spoken and Ireland's cultural traditions are vigorously promoted. The area around Falcarragh, Gortahork and Gweedore has a strong Irish-speaking population, and an Irish-speaking college, theatre and broadcasting station. Children from all over Ireland come to the Gaeltacht to stay in the cottages and houses of the farmers and fishermen to improve their schoolroom Irish.

**FOR HISTORY BUFFS**

**11** *Glenveagh, Co Donegal*
Eviction and emigration are recurrent nightmares that stalked the troubled history of land tenure in Ireland. At **Derryveagh**, one of the most notorious mass evictions took place and was the cause of contemporary outrage. In 1861, John George Adair, landlord of Glenveagh, evicted 244 people from their homes to face the workhouse or emigration after a bitter feud with his tenants and the murder of his land steward. The eviction cottage is marked by a plaque put up by An Taisce, the Irish National Trust, at a spot 1 mile (1.5km) from the Glebe Gallery.

### Errigal Mountain, Co Donegal

**10** Errigal is a distinctive peak, the highest in Donegal, and once recognised you will see it from many parts of Donegal. Its cone-shaped summit rises 2,466 feet (752m) with silver grey scree spilling around the slopes. Avoid the scree, and if you can, climb to the top for a panorama that can stretch from Scotland to Knocklayd in County Antrim, wide over the Donegal coastline and south to Sligo's Ben Bulben. Below lies Dunlewy Lough, and the Poisoned Glen, a sinister name for so pretty a place, but probably deriving from the toxic Irish spurge which used to grow there.

*Take a sharp left, and follow the signs for Glenveagh for 13 miles (21km) on the R251 (L82).*

### Glenveagh, Co Donegal

**11** Glenveagh is a beautiful place, and unusually for Donegal, the beauty here owes something to human hands. Henry McIlhenny, an American who acquired Glenveagh after it had been owned by several other Americans, developed a garden landscape of outstanding planting that never jars with the superb natural setting of water, mountain and bogland. He then gave the property to the nation to become a National Park. His 'garden rooms' are sensitively enclosed, and a walk through the garden follows the route he enjoyed showing to his visitors. The castle is redolent of the house parties for which Glenveagh became famous, when film stars mixed with

*Glenveagh Castle was built in the 19th century, and stands in an extensive and outstandingly well-planned garden*

aristocracy. It bears witness throughout to Mr McIlhenny's fascination with deer.

Glenveagh's origins lie in its use as a hunting lodge, and Ireland's largest herd of red deer still roams the hills in a very important wilderness area.

Close by at **Church Hill** is the Regency **Glebe House**, which has been exquisitely furnished and decorated by Derek Hill, the painter. The art gallery shows selections from the Derek Hill collection and beautiful gardens run down to the lakeside. The **Columcille Heritage Centre** at nearby Gartan, celebrates the life and influence of the saint who is also known as St Columba of Iona.

*From Glenveagh, turn right on to the R251 (L82) for Glebe Gallery, then follow this road before returning left on to the R250 (L74) for Letterkenny. Take the N13 for 22 miles (35km) back to Londonderry.*

Londonderry – Grianan of Aileach **7 (11)**
Grianan of Aileach – Letterkenny **18 (29)**
Letterkenny – Rathmelton **8 (13)**
Rathmelton – Rathmullan **7 (11)**
Rathmullan – Milford **31 (50)**
Milford – Carrigart **10 (16)**
Atlantic Drive **10 (16)**
Carrigart – Creeslough **7 (11)**
Creeslough – Dunfanaghy **7 (11)**
Dunfanaghy – Errigal **16 (26)**
Errigal – Glenveagh **13 (21)**
Glenveagh – Londonderry **38 (61)**

**BACK TO NATURE**

**11** *Glenveagh, Co Donegal*
The peat bog, a familiar feature of the Irish landscape, is a natural habitat not to be taken for granted and is now increasingly protected. A lowland blanket bog lies at **Lough Barra** in a broad valley below Slieve Snaght, and contains pools and rivers. It is an important site for Greenland white-fronted geese, a protected species. There is a raised peat bog in the glacial valley of **Glenveagh National Park**. Here, a rich variety of ferns and mosses grow in the woodland, while red grouse and red deer can be seen on the moorland.

**2/3 days – 163 miles (263km)**

# THE CAUSEWAY COAST

Larne • Glenarm • Carnlough • Glenariff • Cushendall
Cushendun • Fair Head • Ballycastle • Carrick-a-Rede
Giant's Causeway • Bushmills • Portrush • Downhill
Limavady • Ballymoney • Ballymena • Larne

Larne is a busy port at the head of Larne Lough, the terminus for the shortest sea-crossing between Ireland and Great Britain. A 92-foot (28m) replica of an Irish *round tower*, built in memory of James Chaine, 'father of the port', stands in the harbour, but much older are the 16th-century remains of *Olderfleet Castle*. To the north is *Carnfunnock Park*, which has a fascinating garden with sundials and a maze in the shape of Northern Ireland.

Larne marks the start of the celebrated *Antrim Coast Road*. Before it was blasted and forged through limestone and basalt in the 1830s, a formidable feat of 19th-century engineering, communication to the Glens was very difficult, and the Glens folk tended to look across to Scotland rather than to the rest of Ulster. Scottish influences are still noticeable here, particularly in the lilt of local voices.

*A traditional letterbox, near the Giant's Causeway, provides a splash of colour*

*i* At the harbour; Council Offices, Victoria Road

*Take the **A2** coastal road north for 12 miles (19km) to Glenarm.*

### Glenarm, Co Antrim

**1** The Antrim Coast Road is so attractive that it is difficult to resist its magnetic lure, but leave it for a moment to sample the charm of Glenarm, a village that clings to the glen rather than to the coast. The neo-Tudor **Glenarm Castle** is the seat of the Earls of Antrim; its barbican and battlemented, buttressed walls of 1825 rise above the river just as it nears the sea. The village has twisting streets (Thackeray enjoyed their names), pavements patterned in limestone and basalt, a market house with an Italianate campanile and good, modest Georgian houses and shops.

The forest, through the gateway at the top of the village, gives the first opportunity to walk up an Antrim glen. This one is *narrow, leafy and dense with pathways and waterfalls.

*Take the **A2** for 3 miles (5km) to Carnlough.*

### Carnlough, Co Antrim

**2** Carnlough, at the foot of Glencoy, the least dramatic of the glens, has a good safe beach. A railway used to carry lime from the kilns above the village to the harbour, over the bridge that spans the coast road. The bridge, the clock tower and the former town

*Glenarm village, a short way from the sea by Glenarm Glen, has a small harbour that was built in the 17th century*

hall are made from great chunks of limestone. Frances Anne Vane Tempest Stewart, Countess of Antrim and Marchioness of Londonderry, was responsible for many major works, including **Garron Tower**, built in 1848, once a family home, now a boarding school. She is remembered in the town's main hotel, the **Londonderry Arms**, which was built in 1854, and has the feel of a coaching inn.

*Take the A2, following signposts for Cushendall for 9 miles (14km) to Waterfoot. Turn left on to the A43 for 5 miles (8km) to Glenariff Forest Park.*

### Glenariff, Co Antrim

**3** The road obligingly provides a perfect route along this magnificent glen. The bay at its foot is 1 mile (1.5km) long and the chiselled sides draw in the fertile valley symmetrically to the head of the glen. There, the **Forest Park** allows easy exploration of the deep, wooded gorge with its cascades, 'Ess-na-crub' (fall of the hoof), 'Ess-na-laragh' (fall of the mare) and Tears of the Mountain.

**Waterfoot**, the little village at the foot of the glen, hosts the **Glens of Antrim** *Feis* (festival, pronounced 'fesh') in July, a major traditional arts event.

Between Red Bay and the pier are three caves. 'Nanny's Cave' was inhabited by Ann Murray until her death, aged 100, in 1847. She supported herself by knitting and by the sale of poteen (an illicit distillation, pronounced potcheen), or 'the natural' as she called it.

*Turn right to follow the B14 for 7 miles (11km) to Cushendall.*

### Cushendall, Co Antrim

**4** 'The Capital of the Glens', Cushendall sits on a pleasant, sandy bay below Glenballyemon, Glenaan and Glencorp and in the curve of the River Dall. The rugged peak of Lurigethan broods over the

village, while the softer Tieveragh Hill is supposed to be the capital of the fairies. Cushendall owes much to an East Indian nabob, Francis Turnley, who built the **Curfew Tower** in the centre as a 'place for the confinement of idlers and rioters'.

In a tranquil valley by the sea just north of the village is the 13th-century church of **Layde**. MacDonnells of Antrim are buried here, as are Englishmen stationed in these lonely posts as coastguards, and one memorial stone mourns an emigré killed in the American Civil War in 1865 when he was only 18.

*Follow the B92 for 6 miles (10km) to Cushendun.*

### Cushendun, Co Antrim

**5** The very decided character of Cushendun is a surprise. This is a black-and-white village, with an orderly square and terraces of houses that were designed to look Cornish. Lord Cushendun married a Cornish wife, Maud, and commissioned the distinguished architect Clough Williams-Ellis to create a street-scape with style.

A little salmon fishery stands at the mouth of the River Dun, the 'dark brown water'. To the south is **Cave House**, locked in cliffs and approachable only through a long, natural cave. **Castle Carra** is to the north, where the clan quarrel between the O'Neills and the MacDonnells caused the treacherous killing of the great Shane O'Neill at a banquet in 1567.

*At the north end of the village turn on to the road signposted 'scenic route' for Ballycastle by Torr Head. After 9 miles (14km) turn right to Murlough Bay.*

### Fair Head and Murlough Bay, Co Antrim

**6** Paths from the cluster of houses known as Coolanlough cross the barren headland broken by three dark lakes – Lough Doo, Lough Fadden,

**7** Ballycastle, Co Antrim The **Oul' Lammas Fair** in Ballycastle, held every August Bank Holiday, is a remarkable and authentic survivor of a real horse fair with a lot more besides. The streets of Ballycastle are crammed with stalls, including traditional games of chance, and the town is alive with music and fun. Horse-trading lives up to its reputation, and you are more than likely to hear the refrain:

*Did you take your Mary Ann For some dulse and yellow man At the oul' Lammas Fair in Ballycastle – O.*

Dulse is edible, dried seaweed and yellow man a chewy sweet slab.

## BACK TO NATURE

**7** *Ballycastle, Co Antrim* For bird-lovers, a trip on the boat to **Rathlin Island** is not to be missed. Up to 20,000 guillemots, razorbills, fulmars, kittiwakes and puffins can be seen on the sheer rock stacks close to the **West Lighthouse**. Shearwaters can sometimes be seen offshore. Early summer is the best time for viewing.

## RECOMMENDED WALKS

**9** *Giant's Causeway, Co Antrim* There can be few more spectacular walks than the 10-mile (16km) coastal path between the Giant's Causeway and White Park Bay. Magnificent amphitheatres of rocky cliffs, dramatic clefted inlets, basalt sea stacks, an abundance of wild flowers and the company of seabirds add to the pleasure of this walk. A guide will help identify the evocative names for each bay and the historic features, including the remains of tiny **Dunseverick Castle**.

and Lough na Cranagh, which has a *crannóg* or lake dwelling. Fair Head itself is exposed and barren, a place inhabited by wild goats and choughs (red-legged crows). The careful walker can descend the cliff using the Grey Man's Path, which follows a dramatic plunging fissure.

By contrast, Murlough Bay is green and fertile, generous in contours and abundantly wooded. Tradition has it that the Children of Lir were transformed into swans to spend 300 years here. At the top of the road is a monument to the Republican leader Sir Roger Casement, and a row of lime kilns, which would have burned the stone for use in fertiliser, white-wash or mortar.

*After 1 mile (2km) turn right for Ballycastle, then right again on to the **A2** for 3 miles (5km) to Ballycastle.*

### Ballycastle, Co Antrim

**7** Ballycastle is in two parts – the winding main street which carries you up to the heart of the town, the Diamond, under the backcloth of the beehive-shaped Knocklayd, and Ballycastle by the sea, with its fine beach and lawn tennis courts.

At the foot of the Margy river is **Bonamargy Friary**, founded by the Franciscans as late as 1500. Sorley Boy MacDonald is buried here. Elizabeth I found that he eluded all her attempts at capture, but in 1575, when he had sent his children to Rathlin for safety, he had to stand on the mainland helpless while they were murdered by Captain John Norris.

*The rope bridge at Carrick-a-Rede is 80 feet (30m) above sea level, and crossing it requires a good head for heights*

At the harbour is a memorial to Marconi, who carried out the first practical test on radio signals between Ballycastle and Rathlin Island in 1898. You can travel by boat to **Rathlin**, and savour the life of the 30 or so families who live and farm here. The island is a mecca for divers and birdwatchers. Robert the Bruce hid in a cave on Rathlin after his defeat in 1306. Watching a spider repeatedly trying to climb a thread to the roof, he was encouraged to 'try, and try again'. He returned to Scotland to fight on, and was successful at the Battle of Bannockburn.

*i* Sheskburn House, Mary Street

*From the shore follow the **B15** coastal route west to Ballintoy, then turn right, following the signpost to Carrick-a-Rede and Larry Bane.*

### Carrick-a-Rede, Co Antrim

**8** A swinging **rope-bridge** spans the deep chasm between the mainland and the rocky island of Carrick-a-Rede, and if you have a very strong heart and a good head, you can cross it. The bridge is put up each year by salmon fishermen, who use Carrick-a-Rede, 'the rock in the road', as a good place to net the fish in their path to the Bush and Bann rivers. The rope bridge is approached from Larry Bane, a limestone head which had once been quarried. Some of the quarry workings remain, and the quarry access to the magnificent seascape provides some guaranteed birdwatching. It is possible to sit in your car and spot kittiwakes, cormorants, guillemots, fulmars and razor-bills, though you might have to use binoculars to catch sight of the puffins on **Sheep Island** further out to sea.

Just to the west is **Ballintoy**, a very pretty little limestone harbour, at the

*The Giant's Causeway, formed by volcanic rock as it cooled, is 60 million years old*

foot of a corkscrew road. A little further west is the breathtaking sandy sweep of **White Park Bay**. The beach is accessible only by foot, but it is worth every step. Among the few houses that fringe the west end of the beach, tucked into the cliff, is Ireland's smallest **church**, dedicated to St Gobhan, patron saint of builders.

*Take the **B15**, which changes to the **A2** to Portrush, then take the **B146** for the Giant's Causeway, 8 miles (13km).*

### Giant's Causeway, Co Antrim

**9** Sixty million years ago, or thereabouts, intensely hot volcanic lava erupted through narrow vents, and in cooling rapidly over the white chalk formed into about 37,000 extraordinary geometric columns and shapes – mostly hexagonal, but also with four, five, seven or eight sides. That is one story. The other is that the giant, Finn MacCool, fashioned it so that he could cross dry-shod from Ireland to Scotland. Generations of fanciful guides have embroidered stories and created names for the remarkable shapes and places to be found – the Giant's Organ, the Giant's Harp, the Wishing Chair, and Lord Antrim's Parlour. The **Visitor Centre** tells the full story of the geology, the myths and legends, the folklore and traditions.

One story absolutely based on fact is that the *Girona*, a fleeing Spanish Armada galleon was wrecked in a storm on the night of 26 October 1588. A diving team retrieved a treasure hoard from the wreck in 1967, now on display in the Ulster Museum in Belfast. The wreck still lies under looming cliffs in Port na Spaniagh, one of a magnificent march of bays and headlands on the Causeway. A bus service operates from the Visitor Centre down the steep road to the **Grand Causeway**, where most columns reach into the sea towards Scotland.

[i] Visitor Centre

*Take the **A2** for 2 miles (3km) to Bushmills.*

### Bushmills, Co Antrim

**10** This neat village is the home of the world's oldest legal distillery, which was granted its licence in 1608. The water from St Columb's rill, or stream, is said to give the whiskey its special quality and visitors can discover something of its flavour on tours of the distillery.

The River Bush is rich in trout and salmon, and its fast-flowing waters not only supported the mills that gave the town its name, but generated electricity for the world's first hydro-electric tramway, which carried passengers to the Giant's Causeway between 1893 and 1949.

*Follow the **A2** west for 6 miles (10km) to Portrush.*

### FOR CHILDREN

**11** *Portrush, Co Antrim*
Portrush has all the fun of a traditional seaside holiday for children, from donkey rides to candy floss. It also provides excellent parks and recreation facilities, with regular firework displays on Ramore Head. Should it happen to rain, Portrush also has indoor activities, including **Waterworld**, with giant waterslides and games and an indoor funfair.

*Eighteenth-century Mussenden Temple occupies a dramatic site on the headland at Downhill*

## Limavady, Co Londonderry

**13** The Roe Valley was the territory of the O'Cahans, and O'Cahan's Rock is one of the landmarks of the nearby **Roe Valley Country Park**. One story says that it was here a dog made a mighty leap with a message to help relieve a besieged castle, giving this pleasant market its name, 'The leap of the dog'.

The *Londonderry Air* was first written down here by Jane Ross, when she heard it being played by a street fiddler. Limavady was the birthplace of William Massey (1856–1925), Prime Minister of New Zealand from 1912 to 1925.

ℹ️ Council Offices, Connell Street

*Take the A37 for Coleraine, then turn right on to the B66; follow signs for the B66 to Ballymoney, 20 miles (32km).*

## Ballymoney, Co Antrim

**14** A bustling town, Ballymoney remembers its farming past at Leslie Hill historic farm, where visitors can travel through the park by horse and trap. At **Drumaheglis Marina** it is possible to reach the banks of the River Bann, elsewhere a fairly secluded river, and perhaps take a river cruise on a waterbus.

Three miles (5km) northeast, in **Conagher**, off the road to Dervock, is the birthplace of the 25th President of the US, William McKinley.

ℹ️ Council Offices, Charles Street

*Take the A26 for 19 miles (31km) to Ballymena.*

## Ballymena, Co Antrim

**15** Ballymena, the county town of Antrim, boasts as one of its sons, Timothy Eaton, who founded Eaton's Stores in Canada. To the east the hump of Slemish Mountain rises abruptly from the ground. It was here that St Patrick worked when he was first brought to Ireland in slavery. In the south suburbs is the 40-foot (12m) high **Harryville motte and bailey** – one of the finest surviving Anglo-Norman earthworks in Ulster.

Just to the west is 17th-century **Galgorm Castle**, a Plantation castle built by Sir Faithful Fortescue in 1618. Beyond is the charming village of **Gracehill**, founded by the Moravians in the 18th century.

ℹ️ Council Offices, Galgorm Road

*Take the A36 for 21 miles (34km) and return to Larne.*

Larne – Glenarm 12 **(19)**
Glenarm – Carnlough 3 **(5)**
Carnlough – Glenariff 14 **(22)**
Glenariff – Cushendall 7 **(11)**
Cushendall – Cushendun 6 **(10)**
Cushendun – Fair Head 10 **(16)**
Fair Head – Ballycastle 6 **(10)**
Ballycastle – Carrick-a-Rede 6 **(10)**
Carrick-a-Rede – Giant's Causeway 8 **(13)**
Giant's Causeway – Bushmills 2 **(3)**
Bushmills – Portrush 6 **(10)**
Portrush – Downhill 12 **(19)**
Downhill – Limavady 11 **(18)**
Limavady – Ballymoney 20 **(32)**
Ballymoney – Ballymena 19 **(31)**
Ballymena – Larne 21 **(34)**

---

### FOR HISTORY BUFFS

**12** *Downhill, Co Londonderry*
On the **A2** just before Downhill, the **Hezlett House**, built in 1691, is a long, thatched cottage. Restored and open to the public, it is important because of its construction. It was made with 'crucks' – frames of curved timber – which act as upright posts, and sloping rafters set straight on to a foundation of rock. This was a quick way of building in the 17th century. Sometimes Planters brought the frames with them, ready for assembly.

---

### SCENIC ROUTES

**12** *Downhill, Co Londonderry*
The **Bishop's Road** runs over Eagle Hill and Binevanagh Mountain, rising steeply from Downhill. The Earl Bishop had it built to provide local employment in the 18th century. From Gortmore viewpoint the panorama sweeps from Donegal to Fair Head, above the fertile shores of Lough Foyle and beyond to Scotland. The AA has placed a chart showing directions and distances of the views, and another plaque recalls that this was the site chosen in 1824 by surveyors for the most accurate measurement ever then achieved between two places.

---

### Portrush, Co Antrim

**11** Portrush is a typical seaside resort, which flourished with the rise of the railways. It has three good bays, with broad stretches of sand, ranges of dunes, rock pools, white cliffs and a busy harbour.

East of Portrush is a championship golf course, and beyond is **Dunluce**, one of the most romantic of castles, where a sprawling ruin clings perilously to the clifftop, presenting a wonderful profile. The castle was a MacDonnell stronghold until half the kitchen tumbled into the sea on a stormy night in 1639.

ℹ️ Town Hall

*Take the A29 for Coleraine, then follow the A2 for Castlerock, then on to Downhill, a distance of 12 miles (19km).*

### Downhill, Co Londonderry

**12** The feast of magnificent coastal scenery is given a different face at Downhill. Here Frederick Hervey, who was Earl of Bristol and Bishop of Derry, decided to adorn nature with man's art, by creating a landscape with eyecatching buildings, artificial ponds and cascades, in keeping with the taste of the time. He was a great 18th-century eccentric, collector and traveller, who gave his name to the Bristol hotels throughout Europe. Although nature has won back much of the Earl Bishop's ambitious scheme, the spirit of the place is strongly felt, and **Mussenden Temple**, a perfect classical rotunda, sits on a wonderful headland.

Near by is 20th-century man's idea of seaside recreation, at **Benone Tourist Complex**, beside one of the cleanest beaches in Europe, backed by a duneland park.

ℹ️ Benone Tourist Complex

*From the A2 turn left on Bishop's Road for Gortmore, then after 8 miles (13km) turn right on to the B201, then left on to the A2 for Limavady.*

*The Grand Opera House, Belfast, built in 1895 and recently restored, is a masterpiece of Victorian architecture and has a richly decorated auditorium*

[i] River House, High Street

*Take the A2, following signposts for Bangor, and after 7 miles (11km) turn left for the Ulster Folk and Transport Museum, Cultra.*

## Cultra, Co Down

**1** The **Ulster Folk and Transport Museum**, in the grounds of **Cultra Manor**, which is also open to the public, tells the story of the province's past through buildings that have been saved and meticulously reconstructed on this site. Visitors are free to wander through former Ulster homes, which include a thatched cottage, a rectory and a terraced house, and watch demonstrations of traditional crafts. A church, schoolhouse, water-powered mills and many other buildings give a vivid picture of the past. In the transport section, the collection spans the history of transport, from creels used by a donkey carrying turf, through the grand ocean-going liners built in Belfast, to ultra-modern aircraft from the Belfast firm, Short Brothers and Harland. It is worth making an extended visit to this museum, which is one of the best in Ireland.

*Turn left and follow the A2 for 4 miles (6km). Turn right, following the signpost for Newtownards, 3 miles (5km) further.*

*Lismacloskay House, originally built in 1717. It is one of several reconstructed buildings at the Ulster Folk Museum that show what everyday existence was like in the past, bringing history vividly to life*

# STRANGFORD LOUGH

**Belfast ● Cultra ● Newtownards ● Greyabbey ● Portavogie Kearney ● Portaferry ● Strangford ● Downpatrick Killyleagh ● Nendrum Monastic Site ● Belfast**

From the centre of Belfast, the green rolling hills which cradle the city catch the eye at the end of many busy streets, for although this is an industrial city, it is easy to get into the countryside or to the coast. Still a major ship-building centre, it has produced many of the world's famous liners, including the *Titanic* in 1912, and the skyline is dominated by giant twin shipyard cranes.

The city is rich in buildings from the prosperous Victorian age. The restored *Grand Opera House*, in Great Victoria Street, is a masterpiece of Victorian theatre architecture, and opposite is one of the finest remaining examples of a Victorian gin palace, the *Crown Liquor Saloon*.

The magnificent *Palm House* in the *Botanic Gardens* was one of the earliest curvilinear glasshouses. Close by is the *Ulster Museum*, which features a large display of industrial archaeology and the treasure from the *Girona*, a galleon of the Spanish Armada, which was sunk off the Antrim coast (see Tour 21).

## Newtownards, Co Down

**2** A thriving town, Newtownards lies among some of the richest arable land in Ulster. St Finnian founded **Movilla Abbey** in AD540, while the **Dominican priory** was established by the Normans in the 13th century. The hollow, octagonal, 17th-century **Market Cross** also served as the town watch and gaol. The impressive **town hall** was built by the Londonderry family around 1770, and it was the same family that built **Scrabo Tower**, on the hill overlooking the town.

This dominant landmark, standing 135 feet (41m) high, was erected in memory of the third Marquess of Londonderry. The surrounding country park has woodland walks, sandstone quarries and panoramic views.

*i* Council Offices, Church Street

*Take the **A20**, following signs for Portaferry, for 7 miles (11km) to Greyabbey.*

## Greyabbey, Co Down

**3** The village derives its name from the 12th-century **Cistercian abbey** founded by Affreca, wife of the Norman lord, John de Courcy.

North of the village is **Mount Stewart**, a magnificent garden where, enjoying the mild climate of the peninsula, many exotic plants flourish in formal terraces and parterres or in natural settings. Lady Londonderry, the renowned hostess and leader of London society, created it after World War I, and this unique garden is considered one of the finest in these islands. Each garden is given a name – 'Tir n'an Og' (the land of eternal youth), the Mairi Garden, Peace Garden, the Dodo Terrace and the Italian Garden. The lake is particularly beautiful. The house, the early home of Lord Castlereagh,

contains the 22 chairs used at the Congress of Vienna and a masterpiece by the painter, Stubbs, among its treasures. Designed as a banqueting house, the **Temple of the Winds** is an exquisite piece of 18th-century landscape architecture.

The shoreline is an excellent place for viewing birds, including thousands of brent geese that winter on the lough.

*Follow the **A20** for 4 miles (6km) to Kircubbin. Take a left turn on to the **B173** for 3 miles (5km), then turn left for Portavogie.*

## Portavogie, Co Down

**4** Up to 40 boats fill the attractive harbour of Portavogie when the fleet is in. Shellfish are plentiful and local hotels serve a good variety of fresh fish. Seals regularly follow the boats into the harbour to scavenge for food while the catch is being unloaded and the harbour auction is taking place.

*Take the **A2** south for 2 miles (3km). At Cloughey turn left for and follow signposts to Kearney. After 1 mile (1.5km) turn left for Kearney and follow signposts at two left turns for Kearney, about 3 miles (5km).*

## Kearney, Co Down

**5** Kearney is a tiny village of white-washed houses in the care of the National Trust. Once a fishing village, it now offers fine walks along a rocky shoreline that looks across the Irish Sea to the Isle of Man, Scotland and the north of England. Close by is the sandy beach of **Knockinelder**, and south is **Millin Bay cairn**, a neolithic burial site with decorated stones.

At **Temple Cowey** and **St Cowey's Wells**, on a remote and peaceful shore, are the **penance stone** and holy well at a site founded in the 7th

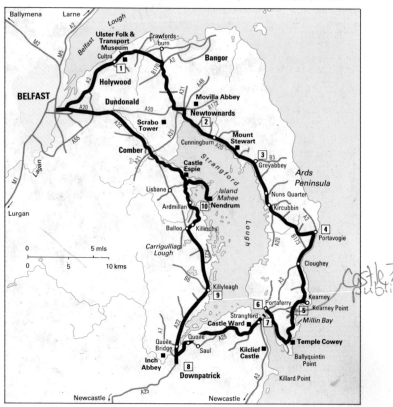

*Mount Stewart House, built in the 18th century, houses a fine collection of art and furniture, and is set in an exotic garden*

century, and later used for worship in penal times. Mass is still said here from time to time.

*Turn left and left again to follow the road around the tip of the peninsula by Barr Hall and Quintin Bay for 8 miles (13km) to Portaferry.*

## Portaferry, Co Down

**6** One of Ulster's most beautifully sited villages, Portaferry's attractive waterfront of colourful terraced cottages, pubs and shops is framed by green meadows and wooded slopes. No fewer than five defensive tower-houses guard the narrow neck of the lough. The **Marine Biology Station**, part of Queen's University, Belfast, is situated opposite the ferry jetty. Close to the tower-house in Portaferry is the **Northern Ireland Aquarium**, set beside a pleasant park, which explains the unique nature of the marine life of **Strangford Lough**. Over 2,000 species of marine animal thrive in the waters of Strangford, including large colonies of corals and sponges in the fast-flowing tides of the Narrows, and sea anemones, sea cucumber and brittle stars in the quieter waters. The lough is host to

large fish, including tope and skate. A regular, 5-minute car-ferry service links Portaferry with Strangford and gives stunning views of the lough.

ⓘ Shore Street

*Take the car ferry to Strangford. Boats leave at half-hourly intervals.*

## Strangford, Co Down

**7** Strangford is a small village with two bays, pretty houses and a castle. Close by is **Castle Ward**, set in fine parkland with excellent views over the lough. The 18th-century house is exactly divided into Gothic and classical architectural styles, the result of disputed tastes between Lord and Lady Bangor. Restored estate buildings demonstrate the elaborate organisation which once supported a country house. A small theatre is used for many events, including a midsummer opera festival.

One mile (1.5km) south, on the A2 to **Ardglass**, a lay-by at **Cloughy Rocks** is a great place for viewing seals when the tide is right. Further south is **Kilclief Castle** and **Killard Point**, at the narrowest point of the neck to the lough. This lovely grassland area with low cliffs and a small beach is rich in wild flowers.

*Take the **A25** for 9 miles (14km) to Downpatrick.*

### RECOMMENDED WALK

**8** *Downpatrick, Co Down*
**St Patrick's Way** passes many of the sites associated with St Patrick around Downpatrick. The saint is said to have landed at the mouth of the River Slaney in AD432, and to have come back there to die. At **Saul**, a small church with a distinctive round tower in traditional style marks the spot where he preached his first sermon. The Way is a network of marked paths, lanes and quiet roads, and is designed to be as long or as short as the walker wishes, from 1 to 7 miles (1.5 to 11km).

## FOR HISTORY BUFFS

**9** *Killyleagh, Co Down*
Driving through the centre of Comber, you cannot fail to see the statue of Major General Rollo Gillespie. Born in this square in 1766, he became a cavalryman at 17, eloped, fought a duel, was acquitted of murder, shipwrecked off Jamaica and attacked by pirates, of whom he killed six. He then settled down to an army life and the list of his battles in Java, Bengal and elsewhere is recorded at the foot of the column, together with his famous last words 'One shot more for the honour of Down', uttered after he had been shot through the heart attacking the fort of Kalunga.

## BACK TO NATURE

**10** *Nendrum, Co Down* A short distance from Nendrum is **Castle Espie Conservation Centre**. When disused clay pits began to fill with water, a sensitive owner quickly realised that this was an important habitat for wildfowl. The careful management that followed has made Castle Espie a haven for birds and an attractive place to visit. Birds which use Strangford Lough can be seen here, as well as endangered species from exotic places. In particular, look for brent geese, wigeon, sanderlings, knot and grey plovers. There is also an art gallery which houses important exhibitions from time to time. A tea-room has views over the lough.

*Above: Portaferry harbour is one of the towers that guard the entrance to Strangford Lough*

## Downpatrick, Co Down

**8** Down Cathedral stands on the hill above the town, while English Street, Irish Street and Scotch Street jostle together below. There has been a church on the site of the cathedral since AD520, but the present unpretentious building dates largely from the 18th century. Ireland's patron saint is reputed to be buried in the churchyard with the bones of St Brigid and St Columba. The Norman, John de Courcy, ordered their reinterment:
*In Down three saints one grave
do fill
Brigid, Patrick and Columcille*
The supposed grave is marked by a granite stone erected in 1900. **Down County Museum** tells the story of St Patrick.
**Quoile Pondage** is an area of meandering freshwater wetland between wooded shores, with fine walks and an information centre. Just north is 12th-century **Inch Abbey**, and to the southwest is Downpatrick race course.

*Follow the **A22** for 5 miles (8km) to Killyleagh.*

## Killyleagh, Co Down

**9** A fairytale castle with soaring pointed towers and ornamental battlements overlooks this quiet loughside village. The Hamilton family has lived here for 300 years, and although the original castle was built by the Normans, its present appearance owes more to the 19th century. Sir Hans Sloane, the physician and naturalist whose collection formed the nucleus of the

British Museum, was born in Killyleagh in 1660 and educated in the castle. It is said that the famous Emigrant's Lament – *I'm sitting on the stile, Mary*, written by Lady Dufferin, a guest at the castle during the Famine, was inspired by the stile at Killowen Old Churchyard.

*Follow the **A22** for 5 miles (8km) to Balloo crossroads. Turn right at the sign for Killinchy, and continue for 4 miles (6km), turning right three times for Comber. After 2½ miles (4km) turn right, following the sign for Nendrum Monastic Site.*

## Nendrum Monastic Site, Co Down

**10** A place of great tranquillity, Nendrum monastic site was established on one of the many islands that are sprinkled along Strangford's calm middle waters, and is now reached by a causeway. The site is one of the most complete examples of a very early monastery in Ireland, and the ruins, in three concentric rings, include the stump of a **round tower, monks' cells** and a **church** with a **stone sundial**.

*Return across the causeway and after 3 miles (5km) turn right for 3 miles (5km) to join the **A22** to Comber, then to Belfast.*

---

Belfast – Cultra **7 (11)**
Cultra – Newtownards **7 (11)**
Newtownards – Greyabbey **7 (11)**
Greyabbey – Portavogie **9 (14)**
Portavogie – Kearney **6 (10)**
Kearney – Portaferry **8 (13)**
Portaferry – Strangford **ferry**
Strangford – Downpatrick **9 (14)**
Downpatrick – Killyleagh **5 (8)**
Killyleagh – Nendrum **14 (22)**
Nendrum – Belfast **15 (24)**

*These enigmatic carved figures are found in the ruined church on White Island. They combine pagan and Christian features and their origin is unknown*

[i] Lakeland Visitor Centre

*Take the **A32** to Omagh for 2 miles (3km) until you reach the signpost for the ferries to Devenish.*

## Devenish, Co Fermanagh

**1** Take a ferry from Trory to get to Devenish Island. Across the silvery water is one of the most important monastic sites in Ulster, founded by St Molaise in the 6th century, although the remarkable group of buildings dates mostly from the 12th century. The **round tower** was repaired in the 19th century, and is regarded as one of the finest in Ireland, beautifully proportioned, with finely cut stone and precision of line. The towers, famous symbols of Christianity in Ireland, acted as signposts, bell towers and places of refuge and retreat in attack, and a safe storage place for treasures during Viking raids. The great treasure of Devenish, the book shrine of Molaise, which is a masterpiece of early Christian art, is kept at the National Museum in Dublin.

On a hill, with uninterrupted views over both loughs, Devenish was such a favoured place for parleys in disputes between Ulster and Connaught that it was sometimes called 'Devenish of the Assemblies'.

*Take the **B82** for 7 miles (11km) for Kesh and Castle Archdale.*

## Castle Archdale, Co Fermanagh

**2** With a marina, caravan sites, youth hostel and recreational activities, Castle Archdale is one of the busiest places around Lough Erne, but it is still very easy to find a quiet place in this country park. In the old estate of the Archdale family is an **arboretum**, **butterfly park** and farm

# FERMANAGH LAKELAND

Enniskillen • Devenish • Castle Archdale
Boa Island • Castle Caldwell • Belleek • Monea • Belcoo
Marble Arch • Florence Court • Bellanaleck • Enniskillen

It is easy to see why Enniskillen is called 'the island town'. Water greets you at every turn – both from Lower and Upper Lough Erne and the River Erne, which flows through the town. The evocative *Watergate* on the lough is part of a castle that was used by the Maguires. It subsequently became a Plantation strong house, and an 18th-century artillery barracks. Now it houses the *County Museum* and the *Regimental Museum* of the *Royal Inniskilling Fusiliers*. The old *Buttermarket* has been made into a very attractive crafts and design centre, and the *Ardhowen* is a beautifully sited theatre with a varied programme. *Portora Royal School* had both Oscar Wilde and Samuel Beckett as pupils. Earlier schoolboys 'playing' in the castle within the school grounds blew it up in 1859 – and it has since been rebuilt.

Enniskillen is now the centre for cruisers that are a popular way of seeing the loughs. Make sure to visit *Castle Coole*, a splendid neo-classical house, the home of the Earls of Belmore, and a masterpiece of the architect James Wyatt. It has remarkably fine interiors and exquisite furnishings.

### BACK TO NATURE

If you are extremely fortunate, you may hear the distinctive call of the corncrake or land rail. Fermanagh is one of the last refuges of this bird, whose population has diminished rapidly in Britain and Europe, as it has become increasingly disturbed by mechanical methods of hay-making. Some experts feel that the complete extinction of this attractive bird is inevitable, but it can still be found here. You are, however, more likely to hear its grating *'crex-crex'* call than to see this rather secretive bird.

## FOR CHILDREN

*Enniskillen, Co Fermanagh*
Much of Fermanagh is ideal for cycling, with gentle hills and quiet roads. Bicycles are available for hire in Enniskillen.

**5** *Belleek, Co Fermanagh*
Older children can enjoy a wide variety of watersports. Windsurfing, canoeing, swimming, sailing and water-skiing are all available at the **Lough Melvin Holiday Centre** at **Garrison**, south of Belleek.

## RECOMMENDED WALKS

There are 114 miles (183km) of the **Ulster Way**, the province's network of paths, in County Fermanagh. A helpful booklet is available.

**5** *Belleek, Co Fermanagh*
A very stiff ascent forms part of the Ulster Way off the **A46** at **Magho**, and gives superb views over Tyrone, Donegal, Sligo and Leitrim. The climb of 365 steps is also rewarded by a fresh, stone-arched well.

**9** *Florence Court, Co Fermanagh* For clearly marked trails of varying lengths, difficulty and interest, try the walks in **Florence Court Forest Park**, through parkland, woods and open moorland.

*This stone-carved Janus figure is found in Caldragh churchyard and may be pre-Christian*

animals of rare breeds. The ruins of the old **castle**, burnt in the Williamite wars of 1689, can be seen in the forest, and the stable block of the 18th-century house is an important part of the park.

The focus of Castle Archdale is the **marina**, where concrete jetties and slipways, built for flying boats taking off for the Battle of the Atlantic in 1941, have been turned to more peaceful use. You can hire a boat with a 'gillie' (a man to help you with the fishing). It is possible to reach **White Island** from here to see the enigmatic **carved stones** that for centuries have puzzled experts and fascinated visitors. Set in the little 12th-century church, they seem to represent biblical figures, with the exception of 'Sheila-na-gig', an unabashed female fertility figure, a strange meeting of Celtic pagan art and Christianity.

*Turn left on to the **B82**. After 2 miles (3km), turn left for Kesh via the scenic route for 4 miles (6km). At Kesh turn left for Belleek, on to the **A35**, then after 1 mile (1.5km) turn on to the **A47** and drive for 8 miles (13km) to Boa Island (pronounced Bo).*

### Boa Island, Co Fermanagh

**3** Two bridges connect the long, low line of Boa Island to the mainland. Just before the bridge at the west end is a track on the left to **Caldragh graveyard**, where there are two uncanny pagan idols in stone. One is called a Janus figure because it is double-faced; the other, a small, hunched figure with hands folded across his lap, was moved here from Lusty

Beg Island. Boa Island, which holds these strange echoes of pre-Christian Ireland, is said to be called after Badhbh, the Irish goddess of war.

*Continue on the **A47** for 5 miles (8km) to Castle Caldwell.*

### Castle Caldwell, Co Fermanagh

**4** Look for the **Fiddler's Stone** at the entrance to Castle Caldwell, set up in memory of the fiddler, Dennis McCabe, who fell out of Sir James Caldwell's family barge on 13 August, 1770, and was drowned. The obituary ends:

*On firm land only exercise your skill*
*That you may play and safely*
*drink your fill.*

The castle, now in ruins, had the reputation for enjoying one of the most beautiful situations of all Irish houses. The fine views are still the same, across a water rich in wildlife, with bird hides that allow an opportunity to catch sight of many ducks, geese and grebe.

*Continue on the **A47** for 5 miles (8km) to Belleek.*

### Belleek, Co Fermanagh

**5** This border village is famed for its fine **parian china**, best known for its delicate basketwork, shamrock decoration and lustre-finish. The range of goods produced by the **Belleek Pottery** has expanded to include designer items alongside the classic patterns, and visitors can tour the 1857 factory, see the best examples of the china and watch exquisite craftsmanship – the result of skills handed down from generation to generation. To this, Belleek offers the lure of a restaurant where the fare is served on Belleek tableware.

*Take the **A46** for Enniskillen. After 13 miles (21km) turn right on the Slavin scenic route for 2 miles (3km). Rejoin the **A46** and after 6 miles (10km) turn right, and follow signs to Monea.*

### Monea, Co Fermanagh

**6** Monea (pronounced Mon-ay) is the ruin of a **Plantation castle**, remote among marshy ground on a rocky outcrop. Built by 'undertakers', or Planters, arriving from the lowlands of Scotland in the early 17th century, it has a Scottish look about it, particularly in the corbelling. The castle was captured by the Irish in 1641 and finally abandoned in 1750. There are still remnants of the bawn wall that surrounded the castle, and an ancient *crannóg* or artificial island dwelling, can be picked out in the marsh in front of Monea. In the **parish church** is a 15th-century window, removed from Devenish.

*Turn left leaving Monea, then left for Enniskillen. Turn right, following signs to Boho for 5 miles (8km), then right again for Belcoo.*

### Belcoo, Co Fermanagh

**7** Belcoo sits neatly between the two Lough Macneans, surrounded by mountains and beside its neigh-

*The 18th-century Anglo-Irish mansion, Florence Court, is famous for its interior rococo plasterwork and furniture. It is set in a beautiful estate*

bouring County Leitrim village, **Blacklion**. The two loughs are large and beautiful.

To the south of **Lower Lough Macnean** is the limestone cliff of **Hanging Rock**, and by the road is the **Salt Man**, a great lump of limestone, which, it is said, fell off the cliff and killed a man pulling a load of salt.

Just north of Belcoo is the **Holywell**, traditionally visited by pilgrims in search of its curative powers.

*From Belcoo, cross the border into the Republic and Blacklion for a very short distance, then cross back into Northern Ireland, taking the road along the south shore of Lower Lough Macnean. Turn right along Marlbank Scenic Loop and drive for 3 miles (5km) to Marble Arch.*

### Marble Arch, Co Fermanagh

**8** One of the highlights of a visit to Fermanagh, the mysterious beauty of the **Marble Arch Caves** is enhanced by a ride on a quiet, flat-bottomed boat through still, dark waters. Over 300 million years of history is here among a strange landscape of chasms and valleys, amid stalactites and stalagmites. The deep gorge of Marble Arch is dramatically beautiful, and it is worth taking time to walk further into the **Cladagh Glen**. Common wild flowers are seen in glorious abundance and variety, as well as some Irish rarities.

*Turn left, then right and drive for 4 miles (6km) to Florence Court.*

### FOR HISTORY BUFFS

**7** *Belcoo, Co Fermanagh*
The narrow strip of land occupied by Belcoo was part of the **Black Pig's Dyke**, a great prehistoric earthwork that formed part of the early boundary of Ulster. The section at the top of Lough Macnean was known as 'The Pig's Race'. The Black Pig's Dyke ran with 'The Dane's Cast' and 'The Worm Ditch', from the Atlantic to the Irish Sea. The Black Pig is a familiar emblem in Ulster folklore. There are many 'races' and paths over which the pig is reputed to have rampaged.

### SPECIAL TO...

Fermanagh offers a variety of quality fishing, unrivalled anywhere in Europe. Its clean lakes and rivers are burdened with fish in a county where coarse fishing competition catches are measured in tons rather than pounds. Game fishing is plentiful, too, with trout, salmon and the unique gillaroo of Lough Melvin. It is essential to check at the Lakeland Visitor Centre about permits and licences.

*Thatched cottages in Bellanaleck. The Sheelin is a craft shop and restaurant*

### Florence Court, Co Fermanagh

**9** Florence Court was the home of the Enniskillen family, who moved from a castle in the county town to the wild and beautiful setting of the present house in the 18th century. The house was named in honour of a new English wife.

The present building, which dates from the middle of the 18th century, is very Irish in character with exuberant rococo plasterwork of the highest order, fine Irish furniture, pleasure grounds and interesting estate buildings. In the gardens is the original Florence Court yew, the originator of all Irish yews.

*From Florence Court, turn right. After a mile (1.5km) turn left on to the A32, then after 2 miles (3km) turn right for Bellanaleck.*

### SCENIC ROUTES

The **Marlbank Loop** runs in a semi-circle round the heights of the Cuilcagh plateau, giving majestic mountain and valley views. Half-way round, a stream, the Sruth Croppa, disappears into the **Cat's Hole**, part of the maze of caves below.

On the scenic diversion from the **A46** on the south side of Lower Lough Erne, the road gains height to afford a fine panorama over the water. This beautiful area is dominated by the cliffs of Magho and the splendid backdrop of Lough Navar.

### Bellanaleck, Co Fermanagh

**10** A base for cruising, with a popular **marina**, Bellanaleck gives a glimpse of the winding, mazy ways of Upper Lough Erne, as its waters thread through 57 islands between Enniskillen and Galloon Bridge to the southeast. Local crafts, including pottery and intricate lace, can be seen at **The Sheelin**, a pretty thatched cottage that also serves as a restaurant.

*Return to Enniskillen via the A509.*

Enniskillen – Devenish **4 (6)**
Devenish – Castle Archdale **7 (11)**
Castle Archdale – Boa Island **14 (22)**
Boa Island – Castle Caldwell **5 (8)**
Castle Caldwell – Belleek **5 (8)**
Belleek – Monea **21 (34)**
Monea – Belcoo **10 (16)**
Belcoo – Marble Arch **5 (8)**
Marble Arch – Florence Court **4 (6)**
Florence Court – Bellanaleck **5 (8)**
Bellanaleck – Enniskillen **4 (6)**

The Ulster-American Folk Park re-creates settings from Ulster and America to illustrate life in the old and new worlds

[i] English Street

*Take the B77 for 6 miles (10km) to Loughgall.*

## Loughgall, Co Armagh

**1** This is one of the pretty, flower-filled villages, surrounded by orchards, in the heart of Armagh, which is known as the Orchard County. The Orange Order was founded near here in 1795.

Close by is 17th-century **Ardress House**, which was given an elegant new look in the 18th century with exquisite plasterwork by stuccodore Michael Stapleton, and some remarkably fine Irish furniture. Ardress still has the feel of a gentleman farmer's residence and the restored farmyard is full of fowl, animals and traditional farming equipment. A woodland **playground** is popular with the children and there is a pretty garden and a woodland walk.

*Follow the B77 for 3 miles (5km), then turn on to the B131. After 2 miles (3km) turn left on to the B28, following the signs for Moy. After a mile (1.5km) pass Ardress House, and immediately after, branch right on to an unclassified road. Turn right again and follow signs for the M1 for 3 miles (5km). At the roundabout, take the B131, which becomes the B34, to Dungannon for 3 miles (5km), then turn left on to the B106 for a further 3 miles (5km) to Moy.*

The Sundial Garden in the grounds of The Argory, near Moy, a 19th-century house in a beautiful setting

# THE HEART OF ULSTER

## Armagh • Loughgall • Moy • Dungannon • Cookstown
## Gortin • Omagh • Fintona • Clogher Valley • Armagh

The ecclesiastical capital of Northern Ireland, Armagh is a gracious and historic city, richly endowed with culture and architecture of centuries of Christianity. Two cathedrals dedicated to St Patrick rise on its skyline, while below, Georgian balance and elegance contrast with winding streets that follow the lines of ancient earth mounds.

Francis Johnston, the best architect in Ireland at the time, built the *Courthouse* and a house that is now the Bank of Ireland, and Archbishop Robinson laid out the Mall in the centre of the city. He also founded the cathedral *Library* and the *Observatory*, and built the *Archbishop's Palace*, now council offices. In the grounds are a superb 18th-century chapel, by Francis Johnston, and a 13th-century friary, and there is a heritage centre in the stables. Along the Mall is the *County Museum*. Armagh has gained a worldwide reputation in scientific circles through the excellence of its *Planetarium*, with highly recommended star-shows, that use the most advanced technology.

## BACK TO NATURE

**1** *Loughgall, Co Armagh*
The **Peatlands Park**, at the Loughgall junction of the **M1**, is the first of its kind in the British Isles, designed to protect bogland and to tell the story of peatlands in an enterprising way. The park is a mosaic of cutaway bogland, with small virgin bogs, low wooded hills and small lakes. The bog is seen as a living archive covering 10,000 years. An outdoor **turbary** (turf-cutting) area gives insight into the process of cutting turf, and a most attractive feature is the **narrow-gauge railway**, originally set up for carrying turf and now a popular way of carrying visitors out on to the bog, thus saving it from the wear and tear of human erosion.

## FOR HISTORY BUFFS

**4** *Cookstown, Co Tyrone*
Northeast of Cookstown is **Springhill**, a lovely 17th-century house with 18th- and 19th-century additions, built when strength and fortification were giving way to comfort and convenience. The Lenox-Conynghams, who built Springhill and lived there for nearly 300 years, were a family of soldiers, and their story, and that of the house, provides a fascinating view of the history of Ireland and further afield. The house has a fine oak staircase, a good library, old gardens of great charm and a costume museum.

### Moy, Co Tyrone

**2** More commonly called 'the Moy', this is on the Tyrone side of the Blackwater river. **Charlemont** lies opposite on the banks of the river in County Armagh. Once one of the most important strongholds of the English, only the impressive wrought-iron gates of Roxborough House and earthworks that were artillery bastions remain. The Moy had one of the most famous horse fairs in Ireland in the 19th century, held in a fine square, where a plaque recalls the son of the village, John King, Australian soldier and explorer.

The **Argory** close by, situated above the river in lovely grounds, is a pleasant 19th-century house, still lit by gas and full of fascinating objects.

*Take the **A29** for 5 miles (8km) to Dungannon.*

### Dungannon, Co Tyrone

**3** A flourishing town, this was once the chief seat of the O'Neills, kings of Ulster for 500 years. Now it is more famous for fine cut glass, and the **Tyrone Crystal factory** is a popular attraction. At Park Lake, a **fishery** offers catches of trout by the pound, as well as an equestrian centre and walks.

Off the main Dungannon–Ballygawley road, at **Dergenagh**, is the ancestral home of Ulysses Grant, President of the US from 1869 to 1877, restored to its appearance of 1880, and set on a farmstead worked by traditional methods of the time.

*Continue on the **A29** for 11 miles (18km) to Cookstown.*

### Cookstown, Co Tyrone

**4** The broad main street runs through a typical mid-Ulster farming town,

but the area around Cookstown has much of interest.

**Drum Manor Forest Park** to the west is small but very attractive, with a butterfly garden, a demonstration shrub garden, a forest garden containing small plots of many tree species, and an arboretum. There is a heronry and waterfowl inhabit the fish ponds.

In the same area is **Wellbrook Beetling Mill**, a water-powered mill used for beetling or polishing, the final process in the manufacture of linen, dating from 1765. Not so long ago there would have been many such mills operating on the Ballinderry river.

The **Beaghmore stone circles** to the northwest of Cookstown are mysterious in their origin and purpose. Perhaps they were formed in the Stone Age or Early Bronze Age for ceremonial purposes, with lines pointing to the midsummer sunrise.

*i* Council Offices, Burn Road

*Take the **A505** for Omagh. After 13 miles (21km) turn right on to the **B46** to Gortin for 11 miles (18km).*

### Gortin, Co Tyrone

**5** This beautiful, sparsely populated area offers a gateway to the **Sperrin Mountains**. Those who want to venture further and even pan for the gold occasionally found in these hills should go north and call at the **Sperrin Heritage Centre**. Gortin has a fine **forest park** with a herd of Japanese sika deer, and the area is rich in good walks. On the Gortin side of the entrance to the forest park look out for a stone seat beside a cool stream, which has the inscription, 'Rest and be thankful'.

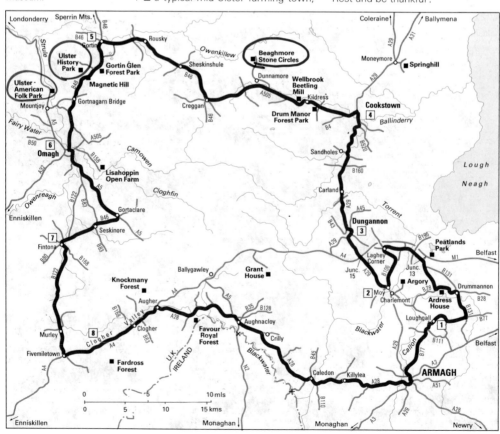

The **Ulster History Park** is here, too, tracing the story of settlements in Ireland from the Stone Age to the Normans. Full-scale models of houses and monuments vividly re-create life in a mesolithic or neolithic home, and other exhibits include a round tower, a *crannóg* or lake dwelling, and a motte and bailey. There is much work to be done in the park, which is still being developed.

Four miles (6km) from Gortin on the B48 look out for the place known locally as the **Magnetic Hill**, which gives the illusion that your car is travelling uphill, when it is really going downhill.

*Take the B48 for Omagh for 9 miles (14km).*

### Omagh, Co Tyrone

**6** Omagh sits high on a hill, spires and the outline of the **court house** giving the town a distinctive profile.

The outstanding attraction of the area is the **Ulster-American Folk Park**, on the A5 to Newtownstewart. It is designed very much in the American style, with costumed interpreters baking bread or spinning by a turf fire. In the **Dockside Gallery** you are invited to sail away to the New World. The park illustrates the two cultures in Ulster's tradition of emigration, from the thatched cottage, representing the Old World (Ulster), to the log cabin, representing the New World (America). One of the most telling exhibits is the re-creation of the brig, *Union*, an emigrant ship. Here, visitors can experience the dreadful conditions, smells and sounds of a transatlantic passage.

*Take the A5 signed for Belfast. After 7 miles (11km) turn right on to the B46 for Seskinore and Fintona.*

### Fintona, Co Tyrone

**7** Fintona is a very quiet little village, once celebrated for its horse-drawn tram. The **Forest of Seskinore** is extremely productive, growing high-quality crops of hard and soft woods. It harbours a rich variety of wildlife and game. Pheasant, grouse, partridges, wild

*A reconstructed log cabin at the Ulster-American Folk Park gives an idea of what life was like in America two centuries ago*

ducks and geese are reared here, as well as ornamental species such as golden pheasant and peacocks. Seskinore was once dependent on using horse power to extract timber. Today's Forest Service has brought back Irish draught horses and trained them to this work once again.

*Take the B122 for 10 miles (16km) to Fivemiletown and the Clogher Valley.*

### Clogher Valley, Co Tyrone

**8** Augher, Clogher and Fivemiletown are the villages of the Clogher Valley, and the names roll off the local tongue, being the stations of the old Clogher Valley railway, much loved by Ulster people. You can easily pick out the red-brick halts.

Visitors to the tiny village of Clogher will be surprised to learn that it has a **cathedral**, its importance dating from the 5th century, when St Patrick made McCartan first Bishop of Clogher. The **folly** on a hill to the south of Clogher on the road to Fivemiletown was a mausoleum erected by a newly-rich landlord, Brackenridge, so that 'he could look down on his neighbours who had looked down on him'.

Fivemiletown has a small **museum** and recreational facilities around the lake. The valley has three lovely forests with different attractions – **Fardross**, **Knockmany** and **Favour Royal**.

*Take the A4 for Augher for 8 miles (13km), then the A28, passing through Aughnacloy and Caledon for 24 miles (38km) to Armagh.*

| | |
|---|---|
| Armagh – Loughgall | **6 (10)** |
| Loughgall – Moy | **15 (24)** |
| Moy – Dungannon | **5 (8)** |
| Dungannon – Cookstown | **11 (18)** |
| Cookstown – Gortin | **24 (39)** |
| Gortin – Omagh | **9 (14)** |
| Omagh – Fintona | **11 (18)** |
| Fintona – Fivemiletown | **10 (16)** |
| Fivemiletown – Armagh | **32 (51)** |

## RECOMMENDED WALKS

**2** *Moy, Co Tyrone* An attractive stretch of the **Ulster Way** takes the walker along the banks of the Blackwater from Caledon in County Tyrone through Armagh to Lough Neagh.

**5** *Gortin, Co Tyrone* From Gortin a number of walks radiate over ideal walking country, with panoramic views. Children enjoy the **Burn Walk**, which follows a stream all the way to the heart of Gortin village.

## SCENIC ROUTES

Linking the Cookstown – Gortin road with the Gortin – Omagh road is Gortin Lake scenic route. The blend of loughs, evergreen and deciduous forests, heather-topped moors and the village below create a fine panorama. Features with evocative names like **Curraghchosaly** (moor with the rocky face), the meandering **Owenkillew** (river of the curlew) and **Mullaghbolig** (humped top) add richness to the picture.

## SPECIAL TO ...

If you are very lucky you may catch a game of Ireland's most unusual sport, road bowls or 'bullets', now found only in Armagh or Cork. Players hurl a 28oz (794g) metal ball (it is said that the game started with cannon-balls) on a set course along winding roads. The aim is to get the ball to the end of the road in the least number of throws. Spectators beware! Watching crowds tend to be quickly dispersed by hurtling missiles.

## FOR CHILDREN

**6** *Omagh, Co Tyrone* **Lisahoppin Open Farm** on the hill to the south of Omagh has a friendly, welcoming atmosphere, and children will enjoy themselves feeding the lambs and goats or gently cradling a fluffy chick. They can watch the milking on this large dairy farm and follow nature trails and riverside walks.

**2 days – 106 miles (170km)**

# MOURNE COUNTRY

Newry • Rathfriland • Banbridge • Hillsborough
Castlewellan • Dundrum • Newcastle • Annalong
The Silent Valley • Spelga Dam • Rostrevor
Warrenpoint • Newry

A town of great historic importance in the Gap of the North between Slieve Gullion and the Carlingford Mountains, Newry's strategic position gave it added significance in the 16th century, and it was in 1575 that Sir Nicholas Bagenal built *St Patrick's*, the first Protestant church in Ireland.

Newry boasts the first major commercial canal in the British Isles, constructed from about 1730 to carry coal from Tyrone. The *Victoria Lock* has been brought into service again, and boats can pass up the canal. At the heart of the town is the *town hall*, which actually spans the Clanrye river, and a thriving *arts centre*.

To the west is *Bessbrook*, built as a model mill village by the Richardsons, a Quaker family, which has a proud claim – 'No pub, no pawnshop, no police'. Just south of Newry a torturous drive to *Flagstaff* is rewarded by superb views over *Carlingford Lough*.

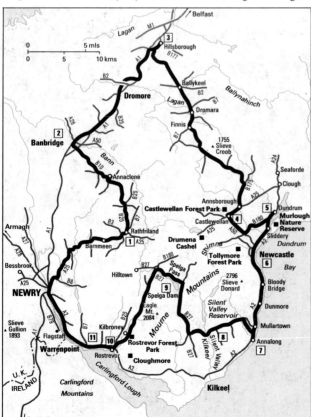

*The ruins of 13th-century Dundrum Castle, which occupies a strategic position overlooking both land and sea*

ⓘ Newry Arts Centre, Bank Parade

*Take the A25 for 10 miles (16km) following signposts for Rathfriland.*

### Rathfriland, Co Down

**1** A quiet village atop a steep hill, Rathfriland commands views over a tranquil valley, where shady roads wind among small farms. This is the country of Patrick Brontë, father of the famous writers, Charlotte, Emily and Anne, and it is said that his stories of County Down were a memorable part of their childhood. The little Drumballyroney school, where he taught, is at the start of the 10-mile (16km) signposted **Brontë Homeland route**. In 1835, Catherine O'Hare was born in Rathfriland. She became the first woman to cross the Rocky Mountains.

*Take the B25 northwards from Rathfriland, turning left on to the B10 for Banbridge, 10 miles (16km).*

### Banbridge, Co Down

**2** The steep hill in the centre of Banbridge was cut through in 1834 to spare the horses on the busy Belfast–Dublin road, and now the wide thoroughfare is divided into three with an elegant underpass. At the foot of the hill, close to the River Bann, is an elaborate **monument** guarded by polar bears. It commemorates Captain Crozier (1796–1848), who was second-in-command of the expedition which found the North-West Passage.

ⓘ Leisure Centre, Downshire Road

*Take the A1 for Belfast. After 11 miles (18km) turn right for Hillsborough.*

### Hillsborough, Co Down

**3** Take time to explore this pretty and elegant Georgian village, full of interesting shops, pubs and historic buildings. **Hillsborough Castle** is the residence for members of the royal family when they visit Northern Ireland, and the permanent residence of the Secretary of State. It stands in a square, not typical of an Ulster village, lined with graceful Georgian terraces. In the centre is the 18th-century **market house**, aligned with a fine gateway and tree-lined avenue to a **fort**. There was a defended settlement here in early Christian times, but the present building was rebuilt as a picturesque toy-like fort in the 18th century by the Hill family, who carefully planned the village through the generations. The Georgian **parish church** adds to the harmony of Hillsborough, and the **forest park** has a lake with pleasant walks.

*Take the road for Newry, but before joining the A1 turn left for Dromara. After 1 mile (1.5km) turn left again and drive for 8 miles (13km) to Dromara. In Dromara, turn left following* *signposts for Dundrum. After 8 miles (13km) turn right and follow the **B175** for 5 miles (8km) to the junction with the **A25**. Turn right for Castlewellan.*

## Castlewellan, Co Down

**4** Another County Down village of steep hills, broad views and quiet tree-lined squares of pleasant terraces, Castlewellan's centre is marked by a solid **market house** and its boundaries enhanced by two handsome **churches**.

Close to the village, the **forest park** covers 1,500 acres (600 hectares) of hilly ground, including a small mountain, Slievenaslat, and surrounds a beautiful lake. A 19th-century **castle**, in Scottish baronial style, stands at its heart. The **arboretum** is particularly fine, and a popular cypress, Castlewellan Gold, which was developed here, has spread the name of the forest throughout the world. Fishing, pony trekking and camping can be enjoyed here, and in the handsome **Grange**, a fine range of courtyards, a **Craft Centre** has been set up.

*Take the **A50** for Newcastle. After 2 miles (3km) turn left on to the **B180**, and after 3 miles (5km) turn left again for Dundrum.*

## Dundrum, Co Down

**5** You can just see the top of the keep of the Norman **castle** among the trees above Dundrum. John de Courcy chose a superb rocky site commanding strategic views over sea and countryside to build his castle in the 13th century, although the name 'the fort of the ridge' goes back to an early Christian defence. The sand dunes below have yielded evidence of Stone Age and Bronze Age settlements, while at **Sliddery**,

just south of the village, an 8-foot (2m) **dolmen** was erected probably 4,000 years ago.

*Take the **A2** for 4 miles (6km) to Newcastle.*

## Newcastle, Co Down

**6** When Percy French wrote of the place where 'The Mountains of Mourne sweep down to the sea', he must have had this part of County Down coast in mind. Newcastle itself is in the shelter of the highest of the peaks, Slieve Donard, but to the south of the town there is barely room for the road to scrape through between the mountains and the sea.

The town is a traditional seaside resort, and offers visitors a promenade, parks, swimming pools and holiday recreation facilities. A magnificent sandy beach sweeps from **Dundrum** to the harbour, and borders the championship golf course, **Royal County Down**. The staff of the **Mourne Countryside Centre**, who provide general information about the mountains, also organise a series of walks for the inexperienced visitor.

Two miles (3km) to the west is **Tollymore**, a magnificently situated and very popular forest park on the slopes of Slievenabrock and Luke's Mountain, in the valley of the Shimna river, with attractive walks enlivened by the picturesque cascades, bridges and follys built by the Roden family.

[i] Tourist Centre, Central Promenade

*Take the **A2**, following signs for Kilkeel for 8 miles (13km) to Annalong.*

---

*Newcastle, a popular resort at the western end of Dundrum Bay, backed by the Mourne Mountains*

### FOR HISTORY BUFFS

**4** *Castlewellan, Co Down*
At **Drumena**, 2 miles (3km) from Castlewellan, there is a good example of an elaborate, stone construction, a **cashel** from the early Christian period with very thick walls. This cashel, overlooking Lough Island Reavy, also has a souterrain, or underground passage, used for storage or as refuge in time of danger.

### BACK TO NATURE

**5** *Dundrum, Co Down*
**Murlough National Nature Reserve** at Dundrum is as beautiful as it is interesting. The dune system here has been cherished by careful management, which makes it a very pleasant place to visit and enjoy. The dunes merge into heathland, and the whole area is bounded by estuary and sea. The range of habitats nurture a wide variety of plants, insects and birds, and wardens lead guided walks through restricted areas. From the magnificent beach, seabirds and seals can be seen, while the inner bay estuary is favoured by a good variety of birds such as redshank, greenshank, brent geese and godwits in the winter. Migrant birds often shelter among the marram grass and sea buckthorn in the dune systems.

## FOR CHILDREN

**5** *Dundrum, Co Down*
At **Seaforde**, a pretty village 3 miles (5km) north of Dundrum, is a **Butterfly House**. It is an extraordinary experience to find that these beautiful, exotic creatures are attracted to visitors and will settle on arms and shoulders.

**6** *Newcastle, Co Down*
Experience warm seawater in the open air at the **Tropicana** in Newcastle, where water fun is provided with games and slides.

## RECOMMENDED WALKS

**6** *Newcastle, Co Down*
There are many excellent walks in the Mournes. Generally they will not be signposted, but walk leaflets are available locally. From **Bloody Bridge**, a short distance south of Newcastle on the **A2**, a path climbs the mountain along the Bloody river, so called because of the massacre in the 1641 rebellion. This is part of the **Brandy Pad**, a track that winds its way through the mountains by **Hare's Gap**, and which was used by smugglers distributing wines, spirits, tobacco, silks and spices, a thriving 18th-century trade.

## Annalong, Co Down

**7** Two rocky clefts shelter the small fishing fleet that uses Annalong harbour, with lobster pots and fishing nets lining the stone pier. A fine **corn mill** right on the edge of the harbour produces flour and oatmeal, and the **Marine Park** is a pleasant focal point on the shore with a play area, boat park and herb garden. A fish smokery and **granite-cutting yards** add activity to the narrow, winding streets and low cottages.

*Return to the **A2** towards Newcastle, then turn left following signs for Silent Valley for 6 miles (10km).*

## The Silent Valley, Co Down

**8** Impressive gates admit the visitor to the vast area of the Silent Valley, which contains two reservoirs and dams which provide water for the Greater Belfast area. The Water Commissioners of the early part of this century planned the landscaping of the reservoirs, and the area has a peculiarly municipal feel about it, with flowering shrubs and formal flower-beds. The splendid mountain panoramas predominate, and today's guardians, the Department of the Environment, have provided walks, a **visitors' centre** and a shuttle bus (you cannot take a car up to the Silent Valley).

*Turn right and right again for Spelga Dam. After 1½ miles (2km) turn right on to the **B27** for Hilltown. After 5 miles (8km) turn left, still following the **B27**.*

## Spelga Dam, Co Down

**9** Just above Spelga is the highest point a road reaches in Northern Ireland, and to the east is a good place for access into the Inner Mournes, the ring of mountains – Doan, Meelbeg, Bearnagh, Donard, Lamagan and Binnian – that shields the beautiful, deep blue Lough Shannagh, and the source of the River Bann. To the north is the pretty **Fofanny dam**, and the Trassey river, where a path gives an approach to the north Mournes.

*Continue west on the **B27** and after 3 miles (5km) turn left and continue for 8 miles (13km) to Rostrevor.*

## Rostrevor, Co Down

**10** Rostrevor is a fashionable, 'arty' place with a flourishing **arts festival** every year. Exotic plants and lush vegetation prove its claim to be the most sheltered spot in Northern Ireland, tucked between Slieve Martin and the temperate waters of Carlingford Lough. As the Mournes descend to Rostrevor the forest pines and conifers give way to native oakwood, which forms a **National Nature Reserve**. Climb to **Cloughmore**, the 'big stone' reputedly thrown by Finn MacCool from Slieve Foye across the lough.

*Annalong has a busy harbour at its heart that is home to a small fishing fleet. On the right of the harbour is an old corn mill that is still in production. The Mourne Mountains are in the background*

SPECIAL TO ...

**8** *The Silent Valley, Co Down*
The drystone walls or, more properly, stone ditches, of the Mournes are an especially attractive feature, enclosing tiny fields, and creating intriguing patterns below the high peaks. Some are single width, seemingly higgledy-piggledy and gaping with holes – no mortar here – others are compact, thick and splendidly flat on top. The **Mourne Wall** is quite different. Solid and massive, it provided employment between 1904 and 1922. The Wall starts and ends at the Silent Valley. Travelling 22 miles (35km), it spans the summits of 15 mountains, and encloses the entire Mourne water catchment area.

*The Mourne Wall, a ribbon of drystone wall, about 6 feet (2m) high, cuts across the mountains for 22 miles (35km). It begins and ends in the Silent Valley*

A real Irish giant is buried in Kilbroney churchyard. He was the tallest man in his day at over 8 feet (2.5m) tall, and died in Marseilles in 1861. Two ancient crosses stand in this churchyard, but a Celtic bronze hand-bell, which was found in a ruined church wall, is preserved in St Mary's Church. A granite obelisk commemorates Major General Robert Ross, who captured Washington in 1814, and ate the dinner prepared for the fleeing President Madison. He died three weeks later in Baltimore.

Rostrevor Forest Park and Kilmorney Park have amenities, a playground, picnic sites and a forest drive.

*Take the **A2** for 4 miles (6km) to Warrenpoint.*

### Warrenpoint, Co Down

**11** Warrenpoint is a resort with a growing port where Carlingford Lough narrows to become an enclosed fiord-like waterway. The Vikings gave Carlingford its name, and this steep-sided inlet must have seemed familiar to them. Carlingford gave good access for their plundering of the rich pickings of Armagh. They may have been the 'foreigners of Narrow Water' recorded in 841.

The English garrison built a stronghold at Narrow Water in 1560 for £361, and the three-storey tower house with battlements, murder hole and bawn wall is a stone's throw from County Louth in Leinster. Narrow Water Castle houses a splendid art gallery, with a permanent exhibition of work by some of Ireland's finest contemporary painters and sculptors and has a regular programme of visiting exhibitions.

Warrenpoint is a traditional seaside resort, with park and bandstand, marina, beach, sports and boat trips to Omagh.

*i* Water Sports Centre

*Take the **A2** for 7 miles (11km) to Newry.*

| | |
|---|---|
| Newry – Rathfriland | **10 (16)** |
| Rathfriland – Banbridge | **10 (16)** |
| Banbridge – Hillsborough | **11 (18)** |
| Hillsborough – Castlewellan | **22 (35)** |
| Castlewellan – Dundrum | **6 (10)** |
| Dundrum – Newcastle | **4 (6)** |
| Newcastle – Annalong | **8 (13)** |
| Annalong – Silent Valley | **6 (10)** |
| Silent Valley – Spelga Dam | **7 (11)** |
| Spelga Dam – Rostrevor | **11 (18)** |
| Rostrevor – Warrenpoint | **4 (6)** |
| Warrenpoint – Newry | **7 (11)** |

SCENIC ROUTES

On the road from Silent Valley, past Spelga to Rostrevor, look for the red metal gates with round knobs on the posts, which mark the water pipelines. Each mountain has its own characteristics, scattered with firs and pines and rocky outcrops, or smothered with naturalised rhododendrons. As the road dips into dark forest, there is a perfect picnic site at the Yellow river, with imaginative tables in wood and stone in an idyllic setting beside a fast-running stream.

# INDEX

References to captions are in *italic*.

# ACKNOWLEDGEMENTS

The Automobile Association would like to thank the following photographers and libraries for their help in the preparation of this book.

BORD FAILTE 56 Mellifont Abbey, 69 Waterford Castle.

THE SLIDE FILE 50/1 Dalkey Island.

WATERFORD CRYSTAL 69 Master cutter at work.

ZEFA PICTURE LIBRARY UK LTD Cover Ring of Kerry.

All remaining photographs are held in the Association's own library (AA PHOTO LIBRARY) with contributions from:
L Blake, J Blandford, D Forss, T King, G Munday, P Zoeller.